STATUS OF ELDERLY WOMEN IN INDIA

STATUS OF ELDERLY WOMEN IN INDIA (A Review)

Editor

Dr. V. Mohini Giri

GYAN

ISBN: 978-81-212-1190-1

Price: ₹ 850

First Published 2013

Published by

Gyan Publishing House
23, Main Ansari Road, Daryaganj,
New Delhi - 110002
Phones : 23282060, 23261060
Fax : (011) 23285914
E-mail: books@gyanbooks.com
website: gyanbooks.com

Laser Typesetting : Awadhesh Computers, Delhi
Printed at : G. Print Process, Delhi

Cataloging in Publication Data--DK
Courtesy: D.K. Agencies (P) Ltd. <docinfo@dkagencies.com>

Status of elderly women in India : a review / editor, V. Mohini Giri.
p. cm.
Contributed articles.
Includes bibliographical references (p.) and index.
ISBN 9788121211901

1. Older women--India--Social conditions. 2. Older women--Government policy--India. 3. Older women--Health and hygiene--India. 4. Older women--Legal status, laws, etc.--India. I. Giri, V. Mohini.

DDC 305.2620954 23

Contents

Foreword

The neglect of a large population of the country formed by the elderly is the loss of considerable potential as well for the benefit of the future. The demographic change because longevity is increasing the population of the senior citizens. They need to be cared and nurtured, and their potential to contribute to the improvement of the degenerating cultural values needs to be utilised. It is a grave error to ignore these aspects, which must be on the agenda of humane governance, in the national interest.

The increasing pressures of modernity and globalisation tend to relegate the concern of the elderly as non-issues into the background. The pressures on the youth to build their career and meet the greater challenges with corresponding opportunities hardly leaves any margin for them to care for the elderly in their own family; and the increasing growth in the concept of nuclear family, often due to necessity, is increasing the need for policies and schemes for the welfare of the elderly. The need is being realized, but enough is not being done to fulfill it, except by some voluntary organization, which are, obviously, not adequate to meet the entire need.

It is, therefore, heartening to know that the Guild for Service, headed by the dynamic Dr. Mohini Giri has highlighted this aspect of societal significance in governance by bringing out this publication containing the writings of some eminent persons, most qualified to speak on the subject, who have a record of active service in this neglected sphere.

I do hope that this work will motivate and encourage others to work for the amelioration of the conditions of the elderly; and activate the governments to do their part for humane governance.

J.S. Verma

From the Editor

To have served as the Chair of the National Policy for Older Persons was indeed an eye opener. During this period my interaction with several hundreds of organizations and thousands of individuals brought to the forefront the urgent need to change attitudes in our society and also in our policies. Some of the insights from eminent people have been recorded here and an attempt has been made to present the collection of articles to all those who are senior citizens now, many of those who are going to become senior citizens, and the youth who need to respect silver. I am grateful to all eminent writers for having contributed. My grateful thanks to my editorial staff Ms. Deepika Thakur, Ms. Garima Joshi, Ms. Anuradha Bose and to our members Shri. Gautam Sen and Ms. Veenita Nagar.

I hope this collection will be useful to the readers.

Dr. V. Mohini Giri

List of Contributors

Dr. V. Mohini Giri, a leader of the women's movement is the voice of women, specializing in human rights, gender justice and peace in India and South Asia. Chairperson: Guild of Service, Former Chairperson National Commission for Women.

Justice V.R. Krishna Iyer is a former judge of Supreme Court of India.

Murlidhar Chandrakant Bhandare is the Governor of Odisha.

Dr. Sheilu Sreenivasan is Founder President, Dignity Foundation, Mumbai.

Dr. (Ms.) Vasantha R. Patri is a psychologist and a practicing Counsellor.

Mr. Madan Mohan Sabharwal is a glorious example of human values and selfless service.

Dr. Kavim V Bhatnagar, a 1991 batch Civil Servant of the government of Madhya Pradesh. Currently he is on deputation to Invest India Economic Foundation, New Delhi, and consultant to the Department of Economic Affairs, Ministry of Finance and the PFRDA on Pension Reforms in India.

Prof. Prakash Narain Tandon he is currently the President of National Brain Research Centre Society.

Ratna M. Sudarshan is currently Director, Institute of Social Studies Trust, New Delhi.

Dr. Damodar Bachani, MBBS, MD, MPHM, over 34 years of professional experience in health sector in teaching and health programme management at national level.

Smt. Rani S. Nair belongs Executive Director, Pension Fund Regulatory and Development Authority (PFRDA).

Dr. V. Mohan is an internationally acclaimed diabetologist and is the Chairman and Chief Diabetologist of Dr. Mohan's Diabetes Specialties Centre.

Dr. P. K.B Nayar Founder Chairman of the Department of Sociology and of Centre for Women's studies and Director of Population Research Centre of the University of Kerala and Chairman of the Kerala State Education Advisory Board.

Dr. Navin Anand is associated with the United Nations as a Resource Person in a Knowledge Sharing Project of United Nations.

Mr. Mathew Cherian, currently full time as Chief Executive of HelpAge India based in New Delhi.

Zena Sorabjee is the Chairman of the Baha'i House of Worship. She is also the Chairman of the Lotus Charitable Trust and Lotus Hospitals Trust.

Dr. Tahir Mahmood, Member, Law Commission of India, is a renowned jurist specializing in Islamic Law, Hindu Law, Religion Law and Law Relating to Minorities.

Anjolie Ela Menon is one of India's leading contemporary female artists.

Guru Shovana Narayan (Padmashri) is a venerated Kathak Maestro of India and an outstanding dancer 'par excellence'. **Dr. Padma Seth** Lawyer Former Consultant with UNICEF, Member of National Commsion far Women.

1

Wrinkles should Merely Indicate where Smiles have been

—Mark Twain, Following the Equator

Dr. V. Mohini Giri

What a joy it was the birth of my grand-daughter, I experienced a greater pleasure and joy than when I had my own child.

I looked at the mirror, which reflected my silver silhouettes. In contrast, when my own child was born I had black, lovely, long hair, tight skin and a vision that could see miles and miles. But things were different now. This time the mirror reflected a radiant face which was full of happiness and also the silver streaks in the hair almost matched the radiance. Eyes may have lost the vision, but I saw maturity, understanding and contentment in them. I rejoiced in happiness of old-age and thanked God for this precious moment.

Slowly, months turned into years and as my steps became slower and unsteady I would hold the little grandchild's fingers and draw strength from her steady walk and her steady directions. A few more years rolled by........ And when an intellectual discussion would take place it was the rarest of rare privilege of joy to hear the young minds take up issues that were dear to me.

Once it happened when I said that "live-in relationships are fine" and the little voice of my grand-daughter said, "How can you say that nainamma......the institution of matrimony is so sacred and has been coming down since ages. Nainamma you have become too young....how can you advocate free living....!!!? I rejoiced in that remark.

Some other day it so happened that the serial "Jhansi ki Rani" screened on the T.V. and suddenly my grand-daughter commented that the history of 1857 revolution has not been portrayed properly and my heart skipped a beat to know the interest that the young had in young India.

When the whole country was talking about corruption and Anna Hazare's fasts, she would argue and say, "the next generation is not going to be the same, as they have learnt from our generation's mistake and things would be different".

These and many other such conversations kept me young and stimulated in the world around.

The Census of India, 2001 pointed out that the population of our dynamic, ambitious youth (i.e. population between 15 to 59 years of age) is 56.9% of the total population.

For me this is another reason for happiness as this 56.9% population is capable, honest and is going to retrospect on every matter that concerns good democracy, and, we could celebrate along-with the young and feel good.

Who says old-age is a burden!!!?

Who says old-age is not a joy!!!?

A few days ago, I had to go to the dentist to get some of the teeth pulled out which happens with advancing age and the joy I experienced in eating soft-cooked, easily-digestible food was like going back in the years of my childhood. Equally joyful was the soft, lilting music sung by my mother on the tape which put me off in such a heavenly 'ananda' which is difficult to describe.

"Who says that a toothless existence is meaningless!!!?"

Take for example, the tremendous amount of work that can be achieved with a single-minded devotion as there are no external disturbances, no child calling you, not having to go and cook for the family or to take care of the household.

There was a time in my youth when any number of saris, and jewelry would not satisfy me and the one-upmanship when you went to parties of who was dressed better and who looked more beautiful.

Today, I find so much joy in wearing simple things and not having a huge wardrobe and being so happy with what I have. If I am not being too boastful, I would like to add that inspite of my simple living, I often hear compliments that 'your silver hair and your simple cotton attire looks so elegant'.

"What is it that the young feels beauty and happiness all around the elderly?"

During holidays, when I visit my grand-children their joy is tremendous. They call me Santa-Claus and look forward to my visit, not for the sake of the gifts but for those many discussions we have on food, art, politics which give a different dimension and broaden my outlook in my youthful old-age.

During my young days, if the air-condition made the room too cold I had to get up to switch it off, but I find greater joy and satisfaction when I share my grandsons room during my visits to Chennai, and, his concerns about me feeling too cold makes him cover me and also to switch off the ac.......what comfort...what joy....!!!

"I fail to understand why old age should be dreaded? Why are people afraid of old-age?"

Elderly can be such an asset to our country, but it is depressing to see that elderly are thought to be a burden. It is true that retirement is a tradition of old-age. Employment of the elderly is an important concern keeping in mind that employment of the young population should not be jeopardized. Serious deliberations are the need of the hour to make lives dignified and productive for the elderly in the sunset of their lives.

The United Nations General Assembly in 1991 recognizing the significance of the ageing population had adopted certain Principles for Older Persons. These principles emphasized on the following entitlements for the elderly;

- To be able to access food, water, shelter, clothing and health care.
- To have adequate opportunities for employment and income-generating activities.
- To be able to decide the time and the pace at which they want to withdraw from the labor force.
- To be able to access appropriate educational and training programmes.
- To be able to live in an environment that is safe and adaptable to them
- To be able to reside at home as long as possible.
- To be able to remain integrated in the society, to be able

to participate on formulating policies that affect them and to be able to share their knowledge resource with the younger generation.

- To be able to seek opportunities to serve in the community based on their interests and capabilities.
- To be able to form movements or associations of older persons.
- To be able to benefit from family and community care and protection.
- To be able to access health-care so as to regain optimum level of physical, mental and emotional well-being and delay onset of illness.
- To be able to access legal and social services.
- To be able to utilize appropriate levels of institutional care that provides them protection, rehabilitation and social and mental stimulation.
- To be able to enjoy human rights and fundamental freedoms.
- To be able to pursue opportunities to the optimum of their potential.
- To be able to access educational, cultural, spiritual and recreational resources of the society.
- To be able to live with dignity free of mental and physical abuse.
- To be treated fairly regardless of age, gender, racial or ethnic background, disability or other status, and be valued independent of their economic contributions.

* *Source:* UN Website: http://www.un.org/en/globalissues/ageing/index.shtml

UN had also declared the year 1999 as the International Year of Older Persons.

Our Indian Constitution, under Article 41 i.e. the Directive Principle of State Policy, commands the State to make optimum provisions for its citizens irrespective of their age.

Recognizing the changes in demography and needs of the ageing population, the Ministry of Social Justice and Empowerment (MSJE), Govt. of India formulated the National Policy of the Older Persons in 1999. The principal areas which the policy addressed were: financial security, health care and nutrition, shelter, education, welfare, protection of life and property, role of NGOs, importance of media and research.

Taking note of various issues, the policy emphasized that for an individual, life continues beyond the age of 60 years too and that older persons are an invaluable resource for the society.

However, with the changing times, the NPOP policy too became quite irrelevant and un-implementable. After several requests and demands the MSJE conceded to review the policy and a committee was formed and I was fortunate to be made the Chairman of the committee.

After numerous discussions and deliberations between the committee and sub-committee members a number of recommendations were made, so that the policy could be easily implemented. First and foremost, the name of the policy was changed from 'National Policy of the Older Persons' to 'National Policy of Senior Citizens'.

Some of the essential points where the National Policy for Senior Citizens attempts to add to NPOP are as follows:

Provisions of old NPOP	*Recommendations by National Policy for Senior Citizens*
	➢ The new policy has laid special emphasis on needs and mainstreaming of elderly women, especially single women like widows because of the multi-dimensional deprivations they face since the beginning of their lives being women. ➢ Due attention should be given to the elderly residing in rural areas because of the existing poverty. ➢ Promoting 'Ageing in Place' and institutional care to be the last resort. ➢ Promotion of age-friendly and age-integrated society. ➢ Being a signatory to the Madrid Plan of Action and Barrier Free Framework. ➢ Implementation of Maintenance and Welfare of Parents and Senior Citizens Act, 2007.

	➢ Establishment of homes with assisted living facilities for deserted older persons.
Financial Security	**Financial Security**
It aimed to provide old-age pension to all citizens who were 60+	• The aim is to cover every senior citizen under "Indira Gandhi National Old Age Pension Scheme". Additional pension in case of disability, loss of adult children etc. • Promoting 'Microfinance' i.e. provision of financial services to low-income clients.
Healthcare	**Healthcare**
It aimed that the needs of the senior citizens to be given high priority. Healthcare would be provided mainly by primary health-care.	• Special screening of 80+ population • Rashtriya Swasthya Bima Yojana (RSBY) to be universalized • Increased focus on mental health and early detection of dementia and Alzheimer's disease. • Expansion of National Programme for Health care of the Elderly (NPHCE) • Focus on health of older women.

Safety and Security The aim here was to protect the elderly from mental and physical abuse.	**Safety and Security** • Promotion of community awareness and policing. • Creating awareness about help-lines, legal aid and other measures.
Housing The aim here was to ensure safe and appropriate shelter to the elderly keeping in mind their mobility and comfort.	**Housing** • Emphasise on age-friendly, barrier- free access • Discouraging segregation of older persons.
Welfare The main thrust was to identify older persons with greater need on a priority basis.	**Welfare** • Provision of universal identity under the Aadhar (Universal Identification Code) scheme. • Larger budgetary allocations in view of the special needs of the older persons.
	Productive Ageing • Creation of Directorate of Employment to be created • Age of longevity to be reviewed by the Ministry.
	Multi-generational Bonding • Promotion of multi-generational bonding.

Natural Disasters Emergencies

This aspect was included to ensure that senior citizens have equal access to food, shelter, medical care etc. after natural disasters / emergencies and adequate facilities.

Implementation Mechanism

- Recommendations to establish a 'Department of Senior Citizens' under MSJE
- National / State Commission for Senior Citizens to be set up.
- Establishment of National Council for Senior Citizens

The main aim, of reviewing the NPOP was to update the policy according to the transformations that have occurred, since the last policy was made.

Here, I would also like to recollect my experiences while working with elderly widows at our shelter house for widows at Ma-Dham. According to **"Dimensions of Deprivation: Report on the Poverty levels of Widows of Vrindavan (Survey conducted by Guild for Service supported by UNWOMEN)"**, 54% of the widows were above the age of 60 whereas, the percentage increases to 92% for the age group of over 70. This interfacing of aging and widowhood when coalesces with culture and tradition becomes a crisis situation for the women to face.

Sources of income for the widows' range from singing at Bhajanashrams, doing domestic work to tailoring and candle making. However, when the widows reach old-age, their mobility and physical capability does not allow them to get involved in the labor force and thus they are pushed below the poverty line. Most of the widows had no rights on their husband's property and were unaware of the Indira Gandhi National Old Age Pension Scheme (NOAPS). Majority of these widows have children back at home but, they do not get any financial support from them.

'yaavadvittopaarjana saktah, taavannijaparivaaro raktah
paschaajeevati jarjjaradehe, vaartaam kopi na prichchati gehe'

(As long as someone is fit and able to earn for his family, all the kith and kin attached to him are affectionate to him; but as soon as he becomes old and infirm and his earnings cease, no one cares to enquire of his well-being).

This phenomenon of neglect, is not limited to elderly citizens living away from their families. Those who live with their families, also often talk about how they are living a life of low quality, emotional and psychological support.

In their study, Dr. A.M. Khan and Dr. Smita Handa found out that in-spite of all the facilities available, human touch is what the senior citizens crave for and, that for the widows, this situation gets worse as they have no one to share their feelings with. Moreover, widows tend to face more physical, emotional and psychological abuse as their dependence on their families increases.

The study reported that elderly citizens, from upper-class families, felt more isolated and vulnerable as they were mere dependent on domestic helpers and had less interaction with their own family members.

For senior citizens, who are not financially well-off, it is very difficult to find dedicated staff who can look after them. There is an urgent need for courses in Geriatric care and Gerontology so that not only there are trained professionals who can look after the senior citizens but, also to build up a resource of knowledgeable academicians who know about the issues of elderly.

It is the need of the hour to sensitize people about ageing, as it is something which everyone will go through. Ageing starts right from the day we are born, until death. I would like to tell all those who are old, who are getting older and those who will get old that ageing is not something to dread about, or an end of something. It is just the next step of life and should be lived with zest. But, one should definitely start preparing for old-age, especially in terms of economic independence.

Thus, through this publication I hope not only to address the issues relevant to senior citizens but also to request people to look forward to ageing.

HAPPY
AGEING!!!

2

Gerontic Compassion and Modern Developmental Dangers

Justice V.R. Krishna Iyer

Man's early civilisation was based on agriculture which began in Asia and developed with in industrialization, in the West. Industrialisation, brought in the idea of business and commercialization.

Today, the dominant ideas of progress in development, which in turn made man the slave of star culture, has destroyed the finer values of humanism and peace.

In this context, the best pronouncement was made by Gandhiji:

'The Gandhian concept of development rejects the idea that it should aim primarily at the creation of material wealth or the satisfaction of insatiable, endlessly multiplied needs. 'In so far as we have made the modern materialistic craze our goal,' he wrote, 'so far are we going downhill in the path of progress.'

Justice, Social and Economic, are the basic structural philosophies of our Constitution. The socialist conscience, of our Constitution, has a special concern for the weaker sector of society. Inevitably, the aged claim more liberal provisions because their capacity to earn economically is less and dependencia on others more for sheer survival.

As you grow old, you retire and your income dwindles. Oldage means more chances of illness, medical dependencia and need for more hospitalization resources. In our insular, nuclear tendency the large family system is less popular. The older members become victims of dependencia syndrome. What is more, the tendency of the young to leave home and go abroad, and, earn and live happily a more attractive way of life, while the elderly get more and more neglected. Their dependence on personal or family laws, makes the older sector and their condition more desperate.

While longevity is increasing, voilence against the elderly is also escalating. These factors are adverse to the social lot of the elderly. More the people live to an elderly age, their dependence on younger people becomes heavier, and the younger people in turn, go abroad and adopt ways of life more expensive than before. Their inclination and ability to help their parents becomes less. Unless new laws are made, the existing laws for the elderly become highly distressing. On the whole, a more dynamic and realistic gerontiogical jurisprudence becomes a social desideratum. The law of inheritance and succession or divorce, do not comprehensively provide an obligation to maintain elderly relatives. The Muslim law does not provide for maintenance for the divorcee and the law made in this regard during Rajiv Gandhi's time, became controversial. We need therefore, a law of maintenance which will take care of poor relations. A socialist conscience must orient the matrimonial law. Even after marriage, the obligation to maintain indigent parents, must be available for the old relations.

Destitution is spreading in our communities. Destitute children are growing in numbers and cases of children being sold, are becoming frequent. Such circumstances call for legislative activism. Our society is socialist and poverty is becoming a crime :- as G.B. Shaw puts it:

"The greatest of evils and the worst of crimes is poverty."

So, we require a welfare legislation which will take care of needy people, deprived of resources. The State has to undertake the creation of Social Welfare Department where every person, without means of livelihood, must be able to claim from the Welfare Department enough grants to sustain and survive. This must be made a fundamental right. Free education and hospitalisation of children must be made a right, even if the institution is private, because we are republic, socialist and there is already a constitutional provision for free education.

The Preamble, to our Constitution, has been interpreted to hold an integral place in the Constitution and so socialism becomes an implied dimension of Law, in India. In this perspective, it is appropriate to enact fiscal legislation providing for Poverty Elimination Tax, something adverse to Wealth Tax.

Money and profit are the negative values worshiped by modern man. This has isolated him from the old idea of family togetherness and insulation. The old man is no longer respected, although, the population of elderly people is substantially high today. If humanism and compassion are loosing their importance, divinity suffers barbarity. The time has come for a new culture of gerontics to claim a high place in civilised life.

3

Senior Citizens: Justice with Compassion

M.C. Bhandare

Eight years ago, when I was 75, I told a story to my golfing friends:

"I sent an e-mail to God. 'Oh! God, if there is no golf in heaven, I am not coming.' Many senior members sitting in the audience immediately rose from their seats to ask me whether I was going to hell. I replied to them, 'Would there be a golf course in hell?' 'Don't worry', then I told them, 'God has replied to my e-mail, which reads: 'Dear Murli, I have ordered a perfect heavenly golf course. However, it will take 25 years more to complete." God wishes me to live at least 100 years. And God's wish is not confined to me; the same applies to people all over the world. In 2005, there were about 265,000 centenarians in the world and by 2050, the number is projected to increase 14-fold to 3.7 million. In USA alone, there were 70, 490 centenarians and in Japan 44,449, as on 1st September 2010.

India is a youthful nation; 55% of its population is below the age of 25 years. However, the situation will change in the coming decades. The world is witnessing an unprecedented demographic transformation. According to UN estimates, the number of persons aged 60 years and above, will increase from about 600 million in 2000 to almost 2 billion by the year 2050 and, the ratio of persons aged 60 years and above, is expected to double from the present 10% to 21%. The increase will be most rapid in developing countries where the older population is expected to multiply during the next 50 years. All societies will experience this demographic change. This transformation throws a challenge to all our societies, to promote and increase opportunities for elder persons to realize their potential to participate fully in all aspects of life and society.

Old age is the last age in a human being's life. It marks the end of the life cycle. We remember Jaques, the melancholy character in William Shakespeare's play 'As You Like It', who compares the world to a stage and life to a play. In a speech, he describes the seven ages of a man's life: as an infant, a schoolboy, a lover, a soldier, a judge, an old man and a man passing through what he says 'second childhood.' In the sixth age, man appears in 'lean and slipper'd pantaloon', with 'spectacles on nose and pouch on side', and his 'big manly voice, turning again toward childish treble.' In the last age, it is mere oblivion and he is left 'sans teeth, sans eyes, sans taste, sans everything.' Eventually, death brings an end to his long and eventful life.

Old age brings a general physical decline: wrinkles appear on the skin; hair colour changes to gray or white and is often associated with hair loss; eyesight fails and hearing diminishes. Hypertension, cardiac problems, diabetes, neck, back, knee, shoulder and joint pains, kidney infections, cancer, tuberculosis and eye problems are some of the ailments that generally affect senior citizens. The World Health Organization (WHO) estimates that about 75% of deaths of people over the age of 65 in industrialized countries, are due to heart diseases, cancer and cerebro-vascular diseases. Osteoporosis and associated bone fractures, which affect many women due to post-menopausal bone loss, also claims the lives of many senior citizens. These diseases require proper and in some cases prolonged treatment. Senior citizens are also susceptible to a variety of mental illnesses. They become less agile; their ability to think reduces and memory fades. Quite a few of them suffer from Alzheimer's disease or brain disorder. Health hazards torment them, leading to loss of control over body and mind.

In old age, one's physical strength deteriorates, enthusiasm lessens, energy reduces and mental stability diminishes; one's power to earn money decreases; negligence on the part of youngsters increases the agony. As one becomes prone to diseases, syndromes and sickness, one is often considered an economic liability and a social burden. Old age is considered an undesirable, problem-ridden stage of life, which one is destined to pass through if one lives longer.

The rise in number of older people has posed a serious problem to all nations. The problem is really acute in the developed societies of Japan, Hong Kong, Iceland, Switzerland, Australia, Spain, Sweden and several other countries. With the spread of awareness and availability of better healthcare facilities, human longevity has increased also in Asian and African countries.

Two factors contribute to the rise in ageing population world-wide—increasing longevity and declining fertility. An increasing in longevity raises the average age of the population and results in increase in the number of surviving older people. A decline in fertility reduces childbirth, thus reducing the number of younger people. In the coming decades, in many countries, the number of the elderly (65 plus) will exceed that of children (0-14 years). The following table gives the ratio of the elderly to 100 children in a number of countries.

Ageing Index: Ratio of Elderly to 100 Children

Country	*2000*	*2030 (projected)*
Italy	127	261
Japan	115	231
Greece	114	206
Bulgaria	106	244
Germany	103	187
USA	59	102
China	27	91
India	14	38

Source: Ashish Bose, "Our Ageing World: More Ageing than Children", *Power Politics,* Volume III, issue 12 (January 2011), page 46.

The figures for the year 2000 and the projected figures for 2030, suggest that India remains a youthful country for many years to come. This large workforce of our country will contribute to its economic growth. However, if the large numbers of young people do not receive proper education and training to acquire skills, they will become a liability. Hence, there is a need for proper planning, effective implementation and huge investment in education. In spite of the fact that there will be a large youthful population in China and India, in terms of absolute number of the elderly, these two countries will be in the forefront.

According to 2001 Census, there were 77 million senior citizens in India, and, the number has increased substantially, in the ten years that have passed since then. The old joint family system in our country has virtually disintegrated, giving way to nuclear families. Traditionally, the younger people in the family used to look after their aged parents and grandparents. But these days, they just do not have the time to do so. Some send their old parents or grandparents to old-age homes and don't even come to visit them. And, quite a few senior citizens living with their families are reportedly facing indifference of the youngsters. There are instances of elderly people being forced to sell their houses. Many old people do not speak up and suffer in silence to avoid embarrassment.

Government of India has taken steps to address the plight of senior citizens. A National Policy on the Older Persons was announced in January 1999 which identified a number of areas of intervention—financial security, healthcare and nutrition, shelter, welfare, protection of life and property for the wellbeing of older persons in the country. A National Council for Older Persons (NCOP) was constituted by the Ministry of Social Justice and Empowerment, to operationalize the National Policy on Older Persons. The policy is currently under revision.

Indian Parliament enacted the Maintenance and Welfare of Parents and Senior Citizens Act, 2007. Its provisions guarantee and recognize the maintenance, and, welfare of parents and senior citizens. Similarly, other matters such as provision of old age homes, medical care of senior citizens, and, protection of life and property of senior citizens are also mentioned there. This is an overriding Act.

Chapter II of the Act deals with the maintenance of parents and senior citizens.

- The obligation of the children or relative, as the case may be, to maintain a senior citizen extends to the needs of such citizen so that, the senior citizen may lead a normal life [4(2)]. It is also the obligation of the children to maintain his or her father or mother or both, as the case may be [4(3)].
- Any person being a relative of a senior citizen and having sufficient means shall maintain such senior citizen provided he is in possession of the property of such senior

citizen or he would inherit the property of such senior citizen [4(4)].

- An application for maintenance under section 4 may be made either by the senior citizen/ parent or a person/ organisation authorized by him/her, in case he/she is incapable, to the Tribunal. The Tribunal may take cognizance suo motu [5(1)]. For securing the attendance of children or relative, the Tribunal shall have the power of a Magistrate of First Class, as provided under the Code of Criminal Procedure, 1973[6(3)].
- The maintenance allowance shall not exceed ten thousand rupees per month {9(2)}. This appears unfair considering the fact that it also applies to a wealthy son/ daughter.

Chapter III of the above Act deals with the establishment of old age homes at accessible places. Such homes may be established, in a phased manner, beginning with at least one in each district to accommodate a minimum of 150 senior citizens [19(1)]. For older people who have nowhere to go and no one to support them, old age homes provide a safe haven. These homes provide special medical facilities to senior citizens such as mobile health care systems, ambulances, nurses and facility of well-balanced meals. The residents live in a family-like atmosphere. They experience a sense of security and friendship when they share their joys and sorrows with each other.

There are more than a thousand old age homes in India; these are run either by Government agencies or by non-governmental organisations. Most of them offer free accommodation. Some homes receive a payment, the amount depending on the type and quality of facilities and services they offer. Considering the number of senior citizens who need safe places to live in, the number of such homes is very small.

Fortunately, model housing complexes for the middle class are growing, for the aged population to live by themselves. In Pune, I have seen housing complexes for senior citizens. They have a guard for their security, a canteen to enable them to have their refreshment, lunch and dinner and appropriate medical facilities. They have formed groups to walk in the morning amd also in the evening. They have provision for swimming and other outdoor activities. There is a park within the housing complex with convenient benches where, in the open space, the neighbours can come together and chat. They do not miss their family members. What is more important is that they are on their own and it is this self-dependence that gives them added vigour to meet the challenges of old age.

Chapter IV of the Act deals with the provisions for medical care for senior citizens. The State Government shall ensure that Government hospitals or hospitals funded fully or partially by the Government shall provide beds for all senior citizens as far as possible [20(1)]. Moreover, there will be separate queues for them; facilities for treatment of chronic, terminal and degenerative diseases, research activities for chronic elderly diseases and earmarked facilities for geriatric patients in district hospitals. Chapter V deals with protection of life and property of senior citizens and Chapter VI with offences and procedure for trial. Whoever, having the care or protection of senior citizen leaves such senior citizen in any place with the intention of wholly abandoning him/her, shall be punishable with imprisonment for a term extending to three months or a fine up to five thousand rupees or both. An offence under this Act shall be tried summarily by a Magistrate [24 & 25(2)].

It is true that the law is in place; but it is our duty to see that these provisions are implemented in true letter and spirit. What is necessary is to recognize the needs of children, differently-abled persons or senior citizens as their rights and not merely matters of compassion or concession. Even now, the courts are looking at several benefits given to senior citizens as mere concessions when, in fact, these are their rights which they are rightfully entitled to for their long and substantial contribution to the family and the society.

There are various schemes for senior citizens like Senior Citizen Plan for Banks, National Old Age Pension Scheme, Hospital Plan in Delhi, Annapurna Scheme and Concessions available in Transport. According to Reserve Bank of India (RBI) regulation, people who have attained the age of 60 or above will get half a percent interest extra and it is followed by all banks. Life Insurance Corporation (LIC) of India, in exchange of a lump sum consideration, pays certain amount periodically, so long as the aged of the annuity is alive. Many civil society organisations are also working hard for it. The Guild for Service, a Delhi-based national-level voluntary developmental organisation, among other things, runs a home for widows called Aamar Bari Ma Dham in Vrindavan, Mathura where most of the inmates are senior citizens. Food, shelter and health security are provided to the widows these, and they are given training in cottage industry skills, so that they could spend the twilight years of life with dignity. Adequate medical care is provided to the sick and to the women who are very old. What is more important is that there is now a general awareness and recognition of the need to take care of our senior citizens. However, the problem lies with the effective implementation of all these welfare schemes.

Senior citizens are often denied their rights. Sometimes they have to fight prolonged legal battles or approach various officials to get their legitimate due. In spite of the priority given to the cases of senior citizens, they have to wait long for justice. A retired professor, after 35 years of distinguished service, gets erroneously and unjustly, a paltry amount of Rs. 2,000 a month as pension whereas her entitlement is much higher, at least Rs. 20,000/- a month. She has been fighting in a court for revision of pension for seven long years with no end to her ordeal in sight.

The United Nations International Day for Older Persons is observed annually on October 1, all over the world, to recognize the contribution of older persons, to examine the issues that affect their lives and to spread awareness among all the generations. Emphasis is laid on the activities that promote the welfare of senior citizens and inter-generational cooperation of the voluntary activities focused on environment, health, education and community service. The World Health Organization (WHO) is actively involved in promoting public awareness and attention on the International Day of Older Persons. Many NGOs are working in this field.

The International Plan of Action on Ageing, adopted at the first World Assembly on Ageing in Vienna in 1982, has guided the course of thinking and action on ageing for over 20 years, as crucial policies and initiatives evolved. Issues of human rights for older persons were taken up in 1991 while Formulating the United Nations Principles for Older Persons, which provided guidance in the areas of independence, participation, care, self-fulfillment and dignity. In 2002, the Second World Assembly adopted the Madrid International Plan of Action on Ageing to respond to the challenges and opportunities of the ageing population in the 21st Century and to promote the development of a society for people of all age-groups.

Ultimately, senior citizens must look after themselves. They should not have a feeling that they are old and merely waiting for the inevitable. The great English scholar and writer Francis Bacon once said, "I will never be an old man. To me, old age is always 15 years older than I am." Senior citizens must also realize that they should be useful to the society not in terms of any employment or position but in terms of a desire to help the society and motivate the younger generations. That way their contribution to the society will be much better recognized.

Old age is also associated with wisdom and enlightenment. Old people are respectfully called seniors, senior citizens or the elderly. They hold a happy place in society where they could relax and enjoy their twilight years watching their children and grandchildren grow. They command attention, respect and affection of the youngsters.

Senior Citizens are a treasurehouse of experience and wisdom. These nation-builders of yesteryears can inspire and guide the younger generations. They have worked hard and made significant contributions to the progress of the nation and advancement of the civilization. The youth of today can gain from their rich experience in taking the nation to greater heights. The society must respect them and learn from their invaluable experience.

4

Ageing Well— A Real Choice, a Practical Option

Vidyaben Shah

Is ageing well a contradiction in terms? Is it not possible for the elderly to feel well while they go through the process of ageing? I will elaborate here, how it is not only a real choice for the elderly that needs to be exercised, but it is a practical option which we in the wider society can make available for our elders, albeit the senior citizens can themselves participate in that process.

As the well known essayist, A.G. Gardiner has said, "The sunset is as glorious as the sunrise." Natural beauty is seen on the faces and in the hearts of the elderly, just as the sunset displays its own natural radiance. The elderly have knowledge, experience and wisdom which is reflected in their behaviour and on their face. With the power of knowledge and skills from years of experience, they can exercise the choice to age well and be an inspiration and source of wisdom for those around them.

How do we, as senior and young citizens make available practical options which make it easier for our elders to go through the process of ageing? The population of senior citizens in India is increasing, and while this presents new challenges that our society has to address, we need to utilise the enormous opportunities offered by the heritage and experiences of senior citizens. The elders are the biggest resources available to themselves as well as to the younger generation.

Historically, in India the old and young always lived together. Today however, the joint family has practically broken down, and the nuclear family is more or less the norm. There are many advantages of a joint family system. Love, warmth and affection for grandchildren, results in the future generation growing up safe, secure and confident. The young in turn keep the elders feeling youthful and wanted. This mutually beneficial exchange helps cultivate a feeling of sharing and cooperation among all members of the family as well as the community. Unfortunately, we are seeing the erosion of this natural arrangement between the young and old. The reasons for the breakdown are many, with people seeking economic opportunities in far-flung places thus, leaving the fold of the extended family. But, the principal cause is a complete change in attitude towards the elderly. When I was a child, I remember the utter respect and regard we had for our parents and their generation, and, the care and diligence and joy with which we would look after them, as they went through various physical and mental changes in their lives. We felt enormous privilege, to share the process of ageing of our elders who had nurtured and nourished us with even greater care and sensitivity when we were growing up. The age of technology and excessive materialism has brought with it objects of comfort but has also caused weakening of human ties.

After working for 5 decades for women and children, I chose to work for older people, having seen senior citizens going through great suffering at the hands of their families, neighbours and the wider community. In some families I saw utter neglect of the elderly, so much so that young members would not give adequate food to their elders. These occurrences were becoming increasingly frequent, to the extent that children would tell their elders to leave what they called 'their' house. I found numerous atrocities occurring in our local community and in my small way decided to work for senior citizens. I was one of the founders of the Senior Citizens Service Forum, an agency which is member of the National Council for Older Persons (Ministry of Social Justice and Empowerment, Govt. of India). It was founded 14 years ago to bring together senior citizens committed to work for the betterment of weaker sections of society. The forum is running a day care centre at Taimoor Nagar, New Delhi, with a view to alleviate problems, experienced by senior citizens in the area, and to provide them with healthcare. All of this work can be carried out quite effortlessly once there is will and motivation and shared aims between the participating elders.

Already there are many individuals, families, agencies and organisations that cater to the needs of the elderly, but there are also several problems with the current situation. On a quick survey of the facilities and systems available to support the elderly, I found a number of barriers and lacunae in our socio-legal systems. This has made the elders highly insecure. We need to develop strategies to gain political, legal and institutional support so that the voice of the older people are heard, but foremost, our elders need to work on developing activities in which they can independently engage, without having to be at the mercy of others. Along with independence and dignity, participation is seen as a key issue in the "United Nations Principles for Older Persons". This means essentially that senior citizens need to realise that only they can bring themselves to participate and engage in personal or public spheres depending on their own inclinations. It is of course necessary that public institutions ensure the inclusion of senior citizens in their programmes, but most importantly it is the elderly who must act to have their voices heard by volunteering individually, or by forming local groups in the community which can represent their views and beliefs. In a small measure, these types of activities are taking place in our society, but I would urge the elders to come forward and actively participate in community activities which will not only restore their lost dignity, but will also keep their bodies and minds agile. The more senior citizens engage, the louder their voices will be and the more varied and rich their ideas of engagement will be, and the more youthful and energetic they will feel.

There can be some simple tasks that senior citizens can take on, such as walking or doing exercise at home, or seeing life with a positive outlook rather than feeling that life is a burden since, the ageing process is rather physical in most cases, they should their minds youthful with positive thoughts. The ageing process, very much depends on inner clarity and intuitive knowledge that to be old is not a bad thing, the elderly do not need to be apologetic or wish to be young, what they are seeking is to be youthful and energetic and positive. This is all a matter for the mind! You will never become painfully old with this attitude.

There is another issue which must not be forgotten. The young also need to remember that a family, a community, a society is made up of a variety of people. It not only comprises different gender groups, religious groups or economic groups, it is also made up of different age groups, and each of these groups is as important as the other. The young cannot monopolise institutions and social structures, they must realise that they will themselves age one day, but most of all living in harmony with all groups of people is the best way by which we will find peace and happiness in our existence. Adjustment on all sides is very important, just as forging links between different types of groups in a society is important for the health of the citizenry, it is also crucial to forge links between the generations, and this can be done only by the willing cooperation of all age groups.

The role of institutions is also very important in forging links between senior citizens and other groups in the society. Though fraught with problems of access, old age pension is now made available by the government. However, provision should also be made for health insurance of the elderly. As average life expectancy continues to increase, we have many more senior and super senior citizens amongst us who may have to tackle ailments and long term health conditions.

A number of laws have been developed in India since independence on economic and social issues, but only recently, a law to safeguard the interests of the elderly, 'Care, Protection and Security for Senior Citizens', was introduced. Experience with laws in our country has been dismal as many are not being appropriately implemented. The law benefiting the elderly, will have meaning only if it is implemented concertedly, and, with care and caution. As in all spheres of life, the issue of gender difference also crops up among the elderly, and the new law needs to cover the interests of the widows and older women, as they are particularly discriminated against or driven out of their own homes. In addition, there should be single gender smaller living abodes which are specifically designed for and made available only to women.

I would like to suggest some key themes, on which individual elders and groups of senior citizens must set aims and objectives and develop action plans to achieve these objectives:

1. Form a local group of the elderly involving an individual for whom it is 'natural' to co-ordinate activities of the group (you might be that 'natural');

2. Join an existing group of elders in the local community;
3. Determine activities of the group that will engender a sense of safety and security among the members;
4. Develop activities that will help to actively engage all members, such as walking together; meeting one morning per week for herbal tea; doing light exercise in the park or in homes by rotation; preparing and presenting skits; putting up a drama show; having a musical evening; taking part in ongoing issues affecting lives in the town such as corruption or keeping the neighbourhood clean;
5. Develop new opportunities for learning, such as using the computer, singing, laughing;
6. How to keep healthy, what to eat and drink, how to develop positive thinking;
7. If there is a mobility problem, to determine what steps to take to move around the house or in the neighbourhood;
8. If living alone, then to plan how to not feel lonely and how to make and keep friends;
9. If living in a family, then to decide how to maintain peaceful and happy relationships and what and how much to contribute to the daily chores and activities of the family;
10. Develop ways to make positive contributions in the community, such as not taking part in corrupt activities, not to bribe or accept bribes, how to keep the streets clean;
11. Identifying 'naturals' in the community or being a 'natural' by volunteering one's support to the local community in some of its many activities;
12. If possible ensuring one's financial security as is practicable;
13. We all come with a fixed life span and planning for passing away with dignity is also in our own hands for

which these days we can plan ahead and prepare a 'Living Will' and entrust it to a lawyer or a trusted family member or friend, outlining how we wish to be treated when we are ill and unable to take a sound decision at that point.

In my experience, I found that it was not difficult to volunteer my time to the community. I actually found that it benefitted me more, than what I had to give of myself to others. Working together with others helps us to create a new family in place of the one we may have lost. And, as we find new energy and cheer through the new family, we also become more attractive to people around us including the family we may have lost and we will find our own relatives coming back to us even for advice and support!!As the Bhagavad Gita says, "Whatever good people do, the very thing others also do; whatever standard they set up, the generality of people follow the same" [3:21]4. For those among us who have yet to grow old, it is worth remembering the words of Prophet Muhammad, "For the youth who will honour an elder for their age, God will appoint people who will honour him in his old age."

Also remember that the best solution for all problems in life is a personal solution, and the best institutional arrangement or system that can support us is a local solution, as that takes very well into account our own specific situations, conditions and problems.

I wish all of you elders in our local and wider world, my very best wishes , that you have a youthful life as senior citizens and that you age well, setting a role model for the young and old of our beleaguered world.

5

Ageing is the Underdog of all Causes in India: An Experientital Narrative

Dr. Sheilu Sreenivasan

The concept of 'productive ageing' is premised on solid scientific evidence that ageing is keyed to the level of vigour of the body and continuous interaction between levels of body activity and levels of mental activity. Age-related deterioration, in most mental functions, can actually be reversed. 'Cenegenics' is the latest upcoming practical panacea, in fact a raging fad in cities such as Las Vegas that ensures its practitioner 'Amortality' (Time, April 25, 2011). Research in gerontology and neuropsychology shows that mental activity makes neurons sprout new dendrites which will establish connections with other neurons. The dendrites shrink when the mind is idle. To put it simply, a person who stops solving problems arrives at a point where he cannot solve problems. Lesson: Keep active. If you do, there is no ageing and its dreaded decline. It is a choice in your hands!

To hail academic theories – The "Wear and Tear" Theory; The Neuroendocrine Theory; Evolutionary vs Life History Theory; The Genetic Control Theory; The Free Radical Theory; Waste Accumulation Theory; Caloric Restriction Theory; Productive Ageing Theory – that actually help improve the quality of longer lives we are enjoying today, is not a bad proposition. In fact, such knowledge can actually pepper daily life, and senior citizens can be self-goaded into adopting such "productive" postures. I myself get so excited when I follow up on research on Ageing.

"The field of ageing research has been completely transformed in the past decade....When single genes are changed, animals that should be old stay young. In humans, these mutants would be analogous to a ninety year old who looks and feels forty-five. On this basis, we begin to think of ageing as a disease that can be cured, or at least postponed....The field of ageing is beginning to explode, because so many are so excited about the prospect of searching for — and finding — the causes of ageing, and maybe even the fountain of youth itself' Guarente, L. and Kenyon, C, *Nature* 408 (magazine). Knowledge is the most basic intervention that serves to dispel "ageism" — the falsely held stereotypes and myths about older people.

These are all dominant engagements of the West. In India, we are still in the stage of grappling with food, shelter, medical services, insurance, income security for the majority of the 91 million people 60+. Despite the necessity of such large scale intervention from the government that rules the country, there are still thematic areas that NGOs and groups can engage in. Those will be my themes in this article.

What does one actually "do" in a society where such negative imagery of old people and the consequent discrimination is at its rampant worst? This is the basic problem. Witness, for instance, the plight of Dignitarian EA Abraham (81), Mumbai, who wanted to enrol for a course in a local college to learn Sanskrit. He was denied admission everywhere on account of his age. He therefore took, to working for a Ph.D degree in Bombay University because that was the only possibility that did not have an age bar. He successfully obtained a degree in Sanskrit when he was 75.

Instances of denial of opportunity for productive ageing run into tomes of gerontological literature documented in ***Dignity Dialogue,*** the monthly magazine for productive ageing, where subscribers give vent to their agony, disappointment, disillusionment, and even betrayal.

Provision of structural opportunities to facilitate older people is the challenge we face in India today, as the country's age profile assumes trends common to the greying Europe and silvering Japan. As sociologist Dr Parthonath Mukherjea, former Director of Tata Institute of Social Sciences, said in July 1996, while presiding over our first "convocation" of senior citizens who successfully learnt computer skills in our classes open only to old people, "individual NGO initiatives in providing such top end opportunities are extremely significant in the face of India's demographic trends. More than the government, it is the NGO sector that seems to come up with innovative ideas."

As a social worker and student of sociology, and running services for senior citizens life enrichment, it is my experiential finding that, in India, the educated middle class seniors are very quick to take to the need for knowledge and practice of productive ageing activities. In sharp contrast to the western emphasis on post-retirement leisure, holidays, good food, fun and frolic, Indian seniors are eager to embrace opportunities for social work. The retired person in India places a high premium on working for a cause rather fritter away retired life in pastime leisure and fun.

The proof of the above statement is seen in Mumbai where 663 Dignitarians, in a unique collaboration with the Bombay Municipal Corporation (BMC), have got into the project of ***Cleaning Mumbai with Dignity.***

Their Helpline, for instance, has nearly 200 senior volunteers working on providing companionship services to lonely seniors in Mumbai alone. "Sometimes elder-callers talk for over 40 minutes as they relate their life stories" says Nergish Olia (75), volunteer in the HELPLINE. The volunteers, all over 50, have been able to reach out to abused elders, where children or relatives have harassed them on matters relating to property. "By being there for older people in need of social support, we ourselves are relieved of the boredom and depression said late Metrani (85).

Productive ageing should not be restricted to the narrow limits of gainful work. Second career or post-retirement pursuit should be ideally defined as combining the best of work and leisure. When productivity is broadened to include work beyond participation in the labour force, to embrace activities undertaken with passion, (something you have always wanted to do, but could not in your first career), it assumes sociological significance.

First, it is useful in arguments of the politics of intergenerational equity. Showing that late adulthood is still productive helps to refute the notion that the elderly are only a drain on family/societal resources. Second, there are definite psychological benefits of productivity in old age — such as better health, motivation, cognitive functioning, life satisfaction or self actualisation etc. Third, it has sociological relevance — social integration and participation, instead of living in the fringes of society.

The crowning expressio, of productivity among senior citizens, is self- esteem and dignity. What the senior citizen in India wants is not fame, name, money, or fortune, but dignity. To be not only conscious of it, but also to be seen to be productive, has an enormous amount of value addition to his sense of self respect. When the grandchild sees her grandmother organising her life with meaning and purpose, the former entertains not only a certain pride in owning up the latter, but actively indulges in even exaggerating grandma's busy schedules. The younger generation is happy to be proud children of productive parents and grandparents, who have in a manner of speaking, learnt to look after themselves, and keep themselves busy and engaged in meaningful pursuits. This is our actual finding borne out of personal meetings, correspondence, articles and interviews that Dignity Foundation has had. The senior citizen wants to live the rest of his/her life with self respect, in dignity.

Ancient and medieval visions of ageing as the “renouncing-focused end part of life” is fast changing, making way for the secular, scientific, and individualistic outlook of modernity. This is true of at least the post-independence generation of India which has benefited the first wave of liberal education.

The corollary of recognising older people as potential contributors to the productive capacity of the society is the equally important recognition that they constitute an important market. Not for nothing did ***Wall Street Journal*** declare that "there is a lot of gold in geriatrics" — a potential that remains largely unexplored in India by business entrepreneurs. Insurance, housing, health, holidays and culturally oriented care services need to be tailor-made for the seniors. Till that time NGOs will have to nurture and deliver precious services for leading the seniors into productive ageing possibilities. Await for instance, Productive Ageing Expo 2011 in Mumbai, Chennai, Bengaluru and Pune in September this year and witness the blossoming of opportunities in our own country!

The Govt. is not cognizant of its humungous responsibilities towards the aged of India nor of the ageing demographic ramifications. The subject is complex, very vast and requires specialised knowledge to deal with its dimensions. One does not see signs of any systematic attempt on the part of the Govt, at even comprehending the phenomenon of ageing in the country. (One exception is the National Policy of Older Persons, 1999, now in its revised version with the Ministry). At the Central Govt. level stray thoughts and measures are at best adhoc; neither the ruling classes nor the educated bureaucracy show any symptom of the need to institute studies to comprehend the phenomenon and recommend large scale measures. At the state level, there is total apathy except in one or two states.

Education of the political classes and of the bureaucracy could probably be an agenda for the NGOs for the coming decade. Groups of senior citizens and a handful of NGOs are indeed very active in influencing the Govt. But more sustained efforts and lobbying are required to awaken the sleeping giant and it could very well be a 20 year process. To start with, the well organised NGOs, groups and associations of senior citizens should be raising a united voice a la the trade union movement.

Demanding the statutory right due to a segment of the population is constitutionally a valid right. But making that demand process effective involves planning, strategy, and a united voice. The Govt., as represented by the political classes, understands only numbers. If, 91 million senior citizens of the country somehow find a way to raise a united voice, it could be heard by the Govt. Everything else is a waste. Any amount of polite petitioning is useless, as experienced by Dignity Foundation, for instance. Writ petitions could be half the way. Judiciary could whip up the necessary command to act. It has the power to move the Executive. But the 91 million has to wake up. At least its intelligentsia and spokespersons have to raise the voice.

6

Ageism : A Key Factor in 'Psychological Distancing' and a Barrier to Effective Mainstreaming of the Elderly

Dr. Vasantha R. Patri

Ageism as a term, was coined by Butler in 1969. He associated it with other forms of bigotry such as racism or sexism. Ageism is a form of discrimination or prejudice based on age alone. It is applied to people of all ages. For example, it could be directed to persons who are too young or are too old. However, it is extremely negative in the case of the elderly. Ageism leads to negative stereotypes that have big consequences in terms of how one views oneself and how others perceive the older person.

Ageism is a form of prejudice

Palmore (1990), lists a set of characteristics that arise from ageism:

(a) An older person who falters is described as 'infirm'

(b) Older persons' 'thoughts' are constantly 'interpreted'

(c) The elderly who 'forget' are charged with 'senility'

(d) Older persons are expected to 'accept' the facts of ageing.

(e) Older persons, who miss hearing something are charged with 'getting old'.

(f) Older persons, who show affection to another are charged of being 'dirty'.

(g) Older persons, who express a dislike for something are termed as being 'cranky'.

(h) Older people are described as being 'childlike' even after society has rendered them dependent, helpless and powerless, like children.

Ageism hurts the elderly

The attitudes of ageism are perpetuated in many ways. The media portrayals are generally negative and the language is derogatory. Institutions contribute to ageism by not hiring or promoting older workers, even when they are fit. Welfare funds are often unavailable for the elderly. Insurance companies fail to cover them beyond a particular age and so on.

Service providers contribute to ageism by denying or limiting services to the elderly. The training of professionals also suffers on this count.

Out of these attitudes and orientations, arise several negative myths and stereotypes about ageing.

Ageism is an attitudinal barrier

Illness – The most common prejudice against elders is that most are sick and disabled.

Impotency – Most elders are seen as sexless. Those who show sexual interest are seen as perverts. (Golde and Kogan, 1958). Even physicians who should know better, often assume that sexuality is unimportant in later life (Butler 1975).

Ugliness – Old people are generally viewed as being ugly. The terms crone, hag, goat, fossil, withered, wrinkled etc., all symbolize ugliness.

Mental decline – Cognitive impairment, especially with respect to memory and confusion are associated with age by both the elderly and others.

Mental illness – It is a stereotype that mental illnesses are common, inevitable and untreatable, in most aged. Both the older persons and mental health professionals view it this way, which is why geriatric psychiatry is a low priority choice, and there is little or poor availability of geriatric mental health care.

Uselessness – Since older people are mostly seen as sickly and/or disabled, their usefulness is always suspected. This results in biased retirement, hiring, promoting policies, etc. Retraining is also rarely available to this group.

Isolation – The majority of the old people are seen as isolated and lonely. This creates more loneliness than actually exists.

Poverty – Generally the older group is seen as poorer than the younger group, which is not always the case.

Depression – Because the older persons are seen as sick, disabled, useless, lonely, poor, senile etc., they are also seen as depressed. This is a misnomer, most of the time.

However, in terms of 'political power' the elderly are seen as a 'potent self-interested political force'. Many of the world leaders are in the older group. This is also coming under the scanner, in the 21st century.

Ageism leads to discrimination against the elderly

The Battle of the Ages

The consequences of ageing are similar to discrimination against other groups. The dominant group's negative image includes behavioural expectations and prescriptions. In this way the younger generation seeks to keep the elderly away from themselves. The treatment of the elderly as 'different' yields psychological distancing.

The elderly respond to the prescriptions and expectations meted out to them by the young, with one or more of the following: acceptance, denial, avoidance or reform. (Palmore 1990).

An elderly person, who accepts the negative image, may 'act old', even though it may not be in keeping with his habits or temperament. This results in loss of self-esteem, shame, unhappiness, self-hatred, lowered self-esteem etc.

Denial would mean lying about one's age and lowering of morale. Avoidance can take the forms of segregated housing, isolation, addictions etc.

The reform response involves the recognition of the discrimination and attempts to fight it and/or eliminate it. This includes collective efforts of powerful senior citizens associations, lobbying for change, etc.

Older women suffer from the double disadvantage of both ageism and sexism

In parts of Kerala in a certain community, the girls are married off to wealthy older men, when they are very young. So they become grandmothers in their mid or late 30's. Many of them are also widowed by this age. Such women suffer from both *ageism* and *widowism*. This is a double-bind for such women. Their bodies are 'young' but the 'social norms' force them to think and behave like older widows. This is psychologically crippling to the group. But they are in a trap and do not have an escape route.

Here the stereotypes determine the thinking and behaving

Researchers in England report that women now are opposing the term 'grandmother', as it has familial overtones. Perhaps the ageistic underpinnings also govern the dislike of this description. It is also negative in terms of age connotation.

Ultimately stereotypes are dehumanizing

People are not seen as individuals, but as objects. So, they are denied rights and opportunities.These are observable at the medical and social levels, also. From such perceptions would follow the abuse or cruel treatment of this group.

So, this segment of the population gets devalued significantly. Thus a vital component of the human resource gets lost, needlessly. This inevitably results in marginalizing of this group.

The Indian orientation to aging, is mixed. Culturally older people are venerated, but with globalization and individualization, they are increasingly viewed, negatively. This is more so in the urban setting.

Cross-cultural studies on stereotypes of elderly in the US, Japan, Puerto Rico, Sweden, Greece and England, were compared with Indians. Sharma (1971) found that Indian students held more negative stereotypes as compared to their counterparts. The Greeks were similar to the Indians. Areas of health and income were uppermost in the Indian group leading to prejudices towards the elderly. They were also less open to humanitarian and welfare oriented support. This may be due to the limited resources available in India, as compared with the other countries and therefore the unwillingness to share. Since the elderly are viewed as being on their way out, investing in them is viewed as wasteful.

Technology is loaded against the elderly

Technology and Ageism

Joyce, Williamson and Mamo (2007) propose a powerful thesis to show how technology and science produce ageist notions and uses that hurt the elderly, distinctively.

Science and technology, is the key to the norms and experiences of modern living. Technology can facilitate better participation, or lead to ageist practices and biases. There are three ways in which science and technology can lead to the social construction of ageist ideas and functioning. One is the medicalization of ageing. Health and illness are now being redefined. Medical labels are turning social issues, into illnesses, that require a medical solution.

In a society, where youthful bodies and thought processes are seen as the norm, changes associated with aging are bound to be labeled as pathological. This means turning natural process into illnesses based on cultural and structural factors. Such a construction eliminates the opportunity to challenge ageist biases. Cruikshank (2003) has documented how sociologists and gerontologists have transformed emotional, physical and mental changes associated with ageing into illnesses. So, a normal component of ageing has been reconfigured into a disease, through the use of medical diagnosis and categorization.

Medical care also suffers from ageism

The best example of such a shift is seen in the pharmaceutical production of 'Viagra'. The original meaning of the term is 'increased flow to the genital region'. To use it as a drug, required the nomenclature of a disease by both the medical profession and the public, for wide support. So, conceptually, the shift in men's sexuality was from 'impotence' to 'erectile dysfunction' Fishman (2007). So men, who complained of premature ejaculation, low desire or erectile difficulties, received the disease label. Thereafter, the number of 'sick' men who sought help, increased. It was also found that some of these doctors who prescribed 'Viagra' were consultants to the drug companies that produced these medicines. So, the redefinition of male and female sexuality was provided by bio-medicalization, capitalizing on ageist practices. Frequent sex is an activity of the younger body. So, the model of natural ageing was replaced by mimicking youthful desires and actions through medicalization notions.

Hormone Replacement Therapy (HRT) was another product that tried to alter the conditions associated with ageing. It included menopause. (Palmlund, 2006). This was achieved by defining menopause as a deficiency disease. That these hormones put the women at risk in terms of heart disease, stroke and breast cancer put no damper on hormone uses. The tendency to define menopause as a pathology, remains. This arises from the ageist idea that has the youthful body as a reference. The wrinkled and dry skin is seen as a sign of deviance, through the ageist's eyes. These have to be avoided. So, anti-ageing medicines have emerged as the new faces of bio-medicalization and ageism at work in the laboratory.

Technology design is another place where technology, science and ageism, intersect. Most technologies are, youth and able-bodied-friendly. For example, computers and internet sites are typically in favour of a youthful body and mind. Precise eye-hand coordination is needed to move the cursor. The font size is generally small. Older people find these difficult, if not intimidating.

Health care-rationing is the third area that technology and science meets ageism. (Adams et al 2006). This can be direct or indirect. Direct rationing occurs when certain goods and services are unavailable for people beyond a certain age, for example like insurance cover. Indirect form is subtle and more difficult to observe. Clinicians, organizations and other health care professionals show discrimination in their practice. Disregarding certain problems, not providing all possible treatment options etc., are indirect ageist orientations, at work, in a significant way.

Most pills come in standard sizes. These can be harmful to older people, because of lowered liver and kidney efficiency in elimination that occurs with aging. But, the pill size is left unaltered, because the older users are less important people. This is the subtle presence of ageism.

Health care shows ageism in action

All the three sources produce inequalities in terms of the elderly. This is ageism's cruel face and always strikes at the very roots of all attempts at mainstreaming the elderly.

In India, ageism creates multiple deficits based on gender, class, caste, education/income levels, besides urban/ rural factors.

In America, ageism has multiple disadvantages caused by gender, race and class besides age -Lee and Gupta (2007). All these lead to the exclusion of the elderly.

Davitt (2007) argues that two of the age based public-policies in the United States, namely employment/retirement and housing are, supportive of ageist assumptions of the older group. This model is being increasingly accepted in Indian, now. One should be conscious of this problem when designing policies for the elderly.

In China, the time honoured tradition of valuing the seniors is being battered by the forces of modernization- McConatha and McConatha (2007).

The Turnaround

Since, everyone has added 20 years life span to normal adult life, longevity is the new reality. Universal human rights now have to include dignity to the elderly. The UN revised population projections put India's elderly at 100 million by 2013.

The policies and principles that are in place are largely well – oriented, but they are often not just or equitable. This is also because of the embedded cultural belief that a person is 'old' when the age of 60 is reached. There are ceremonies to celebrate this attainment and thereafter, one is expected to detach from worldly activities and seek the life of an ascetic. This thinking is fully supportive of ageism. It has to be replaced by the notions of productive ageing.

The Insurance Act, Income Tax Act, Provident Fund Act and other measures, would have to be made age sensitive, in terms of the language used and the spirit involved, while caring for the elderly.

Providing training and educational facilities for the elderly, would be a very good step to fight ageism.

Learning is age-free

Technology and science should be mandated to make all gadgets and devices elderly-friendly. The pharmaceutical industry should be directed to make formulations in keeping with the needs of the older population.

Media portrayals that perpetuate negative stereotypes of the elderly should be completely banned. Instead, the presentations should highlight their strengths.

Focus on the capacities of the elderly not their deficits

Any ridicule or derogatory statements of the elderly, should be seen as outrageous. So, advertising and other health care formulations, need to be performance or need based as opposed to blanket age-based.

The paradigm shift from being pathological to being well, is needed

This process would also effectively counter the bio-medicalization of the body and process of aging. Here the traditional Indian systems of Yoga and Meditation and Ayurveda, all celebrate the concept of wellness in a highly positive way and need to be given a big momentum.

Finally, instead of promoting old-age homes and communities of the elderly, all of which are isolating and therefore ageist based, it is worthwhile to convert the age-old Indian tradition of family community life and make them responsive to the new needs of space and elder/child care.

The *Family Hut* is a concept that is based on inter-locking needs. The old and the young, both need to be looked after. So, the old can look after or supervise the caring of the young, even as the young adults care for the old, in turn. All that one needs to ensure is that the young adults and the old adults do not come in each other's way and stifle one another's freedom.

The kitchen is an anchor point that stands for independence and control. So, if the younger and older adults of a family can come up with such an arrangement, wherein, at least symbolically cooking is separate along with a minimal of living space allocation, then the living together-yet apart would occur. This would mean being psychologically separate, but physically close. So, the caring and sharing would occur without treading on each other's lives.

The Patri model of Inter-Generational living

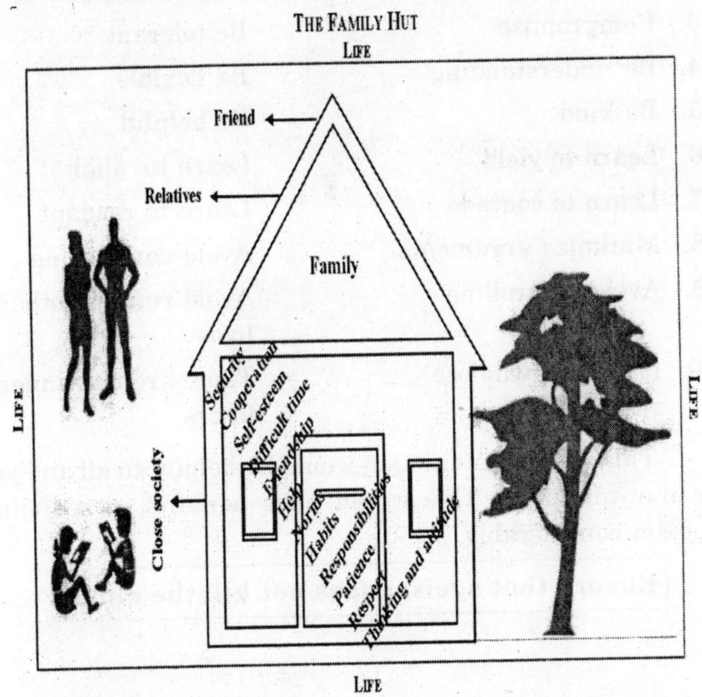

Family is the hut of life. The Family members are interdependent. They make the relationship powerful, due to the interlocking are arrangements.

This would be happy for all concerned and yet the needs of all would be met

In this arrangement, ageism would be considerably reduced as the older people are seen as useful. Being valuable means that the burdensome elements tend to be overlooked.

A few tips for the elderly to manage their own ageist notions—

For the young	For the old
1. Allow for errors	Allow for differences

2. Learn to ignore	Learn to let go
3. Compromise	Be tolerant
4. Be understanding	Be flexible
5. Be kind	Be helpful
6. Learn to yield	Learn to align
7. Learn to concede	Learn to readapt
8. Minimize arguments	Avoid confronting
9. Avoid controlling	Avoid running others lives
10. It is not a win/lose situation	There are no winners/losers

This form of interaction would be helpful to all and yet be non-intrusive. This would have benefits in reducing ageism considerably.

Ensure that ageism does not kill the elderly

7

National Policy and Oldest Old in India

Madan Mohan Sabharwal

Introduction

Scientific advancements, particularly in the medical and nutritional fields, are not allowing people to die early. At present, numerous life- saving devices exist. Life expectancy at birth has more than doubled in the last 60 years and at the same time, the birth rate has been declining. Therefore, the number of older persons is rising steeply. This phenomenon applies to all countries of the world, more so, to the advanced countries of the world. Some countries in Europe, have declining population because there the birth rate is lower than the death rate.

The rate of growth is dependent on the stage of development of the country. The oldest-old population in the more developed regions, is projected to be 3 times as large by 2050 compared to the year 2006; but, in the less developed regions, it will be 7 times as large. In 2006, the oldest-old constituted 13% of the population of the 60+. By 2050, 20% percent of the older population will be 80 years or over.

The population of the older persons in more developed regions of India, is growing at a much faster rate than in some other regions. The demographic profile of India depicts that in states like Punjab, West Bengal, Kerala and Tamil Nadu and Goa the proportion of older persons is higher than the national average and in states like UP, Bihar, Rajasthan and Odisha, it is less than the national average. In other words, economically developed states have higher proportion of older persons than in economically weaker states.

In India also the world trend would be visible in population ageing. According to the Report of the Technical Group on Population Projections Constituted by the National Commission on Population, by the year 2026, the population of older persons in Punjab, Kerala, Tamil Nadu and West Bengal would be 15%, 18%, 17% and 14% respectively of the total population of the state. Compared to this, in the least developed states like UP, Bihar and Rajasthan the proportion of older persons would be 10%, 11% and 11%, respectively.

It is only when people reach an advanced age that they realise that the best asset in the advanced age is good health and not other worldly possessions. The health problems multiply rapidly at the age of 80 years and above i.e. oldest old; which is the fastest growing group of the ageing population. The problems of this group are different from those in the age group of 60 years and above.

Ageing is inevitable. It is irreversible and it is progressive. But, there is no reason why the quality of life should be allowed to suffer to a great deal! In the advancing years, it is fair to expect that old age should be made a comfortable stage of life for all, particularly the most vulnerable of the category.

The National Policy on Older Persons that was announced by Government of India in the year 1999, now falls short of the present- day requirements of older people particularly those in the oldest-old category. There is an urgent need to revise the current Policy to address the urgent concerns of the oldest-old and also devise schemes to implement measures, specially targeted at this group. In India, the family system is still intact and according to authentic sources, more than 90% people live with spouse and families. The number of people living in old age homes is well below 1%. It has been the experience the world over as well, that oldest old live with families. The Policy should capitalise on this strength of our social system and make provisions to facilitate the living of older persons with their families or in their homes instead of institutions.

Demographic Context: India and the World

The oldest old (80 years and over), are the fastest growing segment of the world's population and are increasing more rapidly and at a higher rate, than the population of older persons (60+) and also of the general population. According to the UN estimates, the number of older persons is estimated to increase from 688 million in 2006 to 1,968 million in 2050; while those of the 80+ are expected to increase from 89.4 million to 394 million, in the same duration. In proportional terms, the increase in the total population of the old during the period is 2.87 times, while that of the 80+ is 4.4 times.

The demographic profile depicts that in the years 2000-2050, the overall population in India will grow by 55% whereas, population of people in the 60 years and above age category will increase by 326% and, those in the age group of 80+, by 700% (the fastest growing group as seen in the table). The number of centenarians (aged 100 years and over) is projected to increase 18 fold, from approximately 180 thousand in 2000 to 3219 thousand by 2050.

Years	*Total Population (millions)*	*60+ (millions)*	*80+ (millions)*
2000	1008	76	6
2050	1572	324	48

Source: World population Ageing: 1950-2050; Department of Economic and Social affairs, Population Division, United Nations. New York. 2002.

Implications of Increase in the Oldest Old Population

A vast majority of the 80+ live in rural areas, which have the least facilities for the special health and family care, needed by them. The problems of 80+ are different from those of young old.

Moreover, perception of 80+ about their problems changes rather drastically as the age increases. For example, young and middle-age olds (60-79 years) may be more concerned with their economic needs, and, the necessity to remain fit and independent, while 80+ are often sick, frail, physically weak, vulnerable to crime and dependent on others requiring urgent support measures. They are also often excluded from the social and economic spheres of life. This group should not be treated as a part of homogenous group of all older persons.

Oldest old (80+) females constitute an especially vulnerable group. An overwhelming proportion of this group are widows, who in India suffer multiple miseries - being women, being widows, being poor and having longer agonising years to live than men.

The phenomenon of ageing of the 80+, with enormous load of multiple morbidities, needs urgent attention and consideration. This group suffers more on account of disability, chronic disease, terminal illness, dementia and depression, accidents, falls, nutritional deficiencies, loneliness etc. Some of these diseases have no cure as yet. Furthermore, this group is subject to abuse, as they are financially and emotionally dependent on families and others. It is important to make the 80+, financially self - sustaining. Their pension needs to be improved and there should be provision for free medical aid, particularly for those who are exempt from paying Income Tax. They constitute only about 1% of the total population of India and in absolute number, this is currently around 10 million and will grow to around 53 million by the year 2050 i.e. 3.5% of total population.

The data on living arrangement of oldest old in the rural areas suggests that most of them live with the families of their adult children. The oldest old depend on their children to take care of them, during ill health or any other health related problems. However, the children always are not helpful and in many cases the oldest old depend on the spouse. Many of them face the problem of insufficient food intake as well. Some of them also report economic abuse by the family members.

The other health problems faced by oldest old include asthma, poor eyesight, cold and cough, joint pain and problems related to general physical weakness. Most of the oldest old depend on private doctor/ clinic, community health centre and primary health centre in the area for treatment. There, services have much to be desired and are expensive. The oldest old in the rural areas are not covered by any health insurance scheme and therefore, find it difficult to access health care system.

Although, well - being of older persons has been mandated in the Indian Constitution, under entry 24 in List III of Schedule VII, item 9 of the State List and item 20, 23 and 24 of the Concurrent List and Article 41; there are no government welfare schemes for the benefit of oldest old persons except Indira Gandhi National Old Age Pension Scheme. Besides, in most cases, there are no dependable community support systems that the oldest old can depend on.

Recommended Policy Measures

In light of the demographic facts mentioned above and the socio-economic implications, the following measures are strongly recommended to deal effectively with the challenges that increase in the population of oldest old pose to society.

As already stated that in India, family still provides support to overwhelming majority of older persons. The Policy should go beyond acknowledging the family support and take concrete measures to facilitate and reinforce the continuation of this system. Public - private partnership model should be devised, to deal with the care and other aspects of this challenge. The healthcare system and other public systems should be sympathetic to the special needs of the very old persons and their care givers, and change the procedures to suit the needs. Monetary assistance for the older person is on the one end of the spectrum and care on the other. Health is somewhere in the middle on this continuum.

Money is required for all major and minor expenses till the last breath. Therefore, Policy should address this basic need of older persons depending on their specific requirement. Chronically poor may need full support, but the middle class and high income families may be able to take care of the daily expenses, but not health. So, subsidised healthcare would take the burden off them. Besides, affordability and accessibility should also be kept in mind while designing the health and other care programmes. The issues of care givers, to supplement the efforts of the family in taking care of oldest old, would go a long way in ensuring their 'ageing-in-place'. The Policy should address the critical area of care givers, healthcare professionals and other related activities, to encourage families to care for their oldest old members and ensure a life of dignity and independence to the oldest old.

The following recommendations are more specific in nature and cover almost all major concerns of oldest old in India. These measures if taken earnestly, will go a long way in successful handling of the needs of the fastest growing segment of the elderly population in India.

Economic Security

1. Universal coverage of poor older persons over the age of 80 years under the Indira Gandhi National Old Age Scheme. Additional money to be given in case of disability, loss of adult children and concomitant responsibility of grand children and women.
2. Distribution of free ration under the Public Distribution System to the destitute 80+.
3. Income upto Rs. 10 lakhs per annum to be made tax exempt.
4. Additional (substantial) interest should be given to investors over the age of 80 years by banks and post offices saving schemes. This income should be tax exempt.
5. Legislation for maintenance of parents should be flexible to adjust the special needs of parents over the age of 80 years.
6. Insurance cover should be provided to all older persons over the age of 80, under publically funded schemes.
7. Issuance of Identity Cards.

Health and Nutrition

1. Availability of universal free medical aid for persons aged 80+ years and above.
2. Availability of basic geriatric services in primary health centres, to tackle health issues of rural elderly including six monthly assessment services for 80+, ambulatory individuals to detect medical, social, psychological impairments.
3. Availability of care services: convalescent, rehabilitation, respite, long - term and most importantly home- care service.
4. Dedicated units for ensuring mental health and well-being at all levels of health-care.
5. Guidelines for nutrition in old age should be prepared and disseminated widely.
6. Availability of Schemes for mid-day meals for destitute oldest old persons.
7. Efforts should be made by concerned authorities to deal with disability by introducing technological devices.
8. Public private partnership model should be used to expand, to provide general healthcare in community and specialised services, like palliative care.
9. Extensive specialised training programmes should be conducted to orient the medical and para-medical staff to deal with special needs of oldest-old.
10. Screening of the 80+ individuals in the villages and urban areas by the PHC nurse/health worker, twice a year.

Protection and Abuse

1. Stringent legislation needed to protect the life and property of oldest old. Suitable amendments should be made to the existing legislation and new laws formulated for the purpose.
2. Police should be sensitized to deal effectively with cases of abuse of oldest old.
3. Community and grass-root level NGOs should be trained to recognise abuse and take action.
4. Counselling centres should be available to deal with family conflicts.

General

1. The government at all levels should be mindful of the concerns of this specifically vulnerable segment of the ageing population while framing laws, policies and programme.
2. The NGOs and community based organisations should be encouraged to participate in the programmes meant for oldest old.
3. The general review process of the policy should highlight the progress made, for the benefit of vulnerable segments of the ageing population particularly the oldest old.
4. Specific programmes of intergenerational bonding should be designed and implemented, to increase the sensitivity of the younger generation to the oldest old.

Conclusion

In old times, very few people lived to the ripe old age of 80 years or above and it was considered a matter of pride. But, now a large part of the population is easily going to reach that age, and with changing social and economic system, face new challenges of care and maintenance, as it may not always be completely independent in all respects. Therefore, the Policy should take note of this demographic fact and treat this as an urgent concern and start taking steps to deal effectively with it in future. We could learn from the experiences of the Asian countries like Japan etc. with a mix of formal and informal care, rather than the Western countries that heavily institutionalised old age care and are now finding it unsustainable.

With declining birth rate and increasing longevity, we are all likely to face a situation that oldest old will be taken care of by the young old. Therefore, it is imperative that the Policy ensures that the older persons remain active and healthy, for as long as possible. This will help the young old to take care of the oldest old and the oldest old would not be completely dependent. Very few would be bed-ridden or suffer from dementia and other such diseases that require extensive care. However, there should be institutions to assist these young old care givers, to de-stress and take on the responsibility.

8

Human Rights of Older Women Power of Old Age

Dr. V. Mohini Giri

Long long ago, when women were really desperate for social justice and equality, it was Hilary Clinton at the 1st World Conference at Beijing for women, gave a call "Women Rights are Human Rights". Today it is time that we give a clarion call for "Elderly Rights are Human Rights".

The elderly are a precious asset to the country. A significant feature of the demographic change is the progressive increase in the number of elderly persons. According to the 2001 census, the elderly contributed 7% of the total population. Almost, 75% live in rural areas.

Of course, one is bound to look after ones parents but due to unavoidable reasons like poverty, marginalization, isolation, insecurity and generation gap there is a stress in joint and extended families.

Year after, year as we all celebrate the World Elderly Day, we will be failing in our duty if we do not find steps to improve the quality of the life of senior citizens and also give them the due dignity. Since, we are living in a global world, I would like to point out that these problems pose serious threats to all nations. The problem is really acute in the developed societies of Japan, Hong Kong, Iceland, Switzerland, Australia, Spain, Sweden and several other countries. With the spread of awareness and availability of better healthcare facilities, human longevity has increased also in Asian and African countries. Two factors contribute to the rise in ageing population world-wide-increasing longevity which raises the average age of the population and results in increasing the number of surviving older people. A decline in fertility reduces childbirth, thus, reducing the number of younger people. In the coming decades, in many countries, the number of the elderly (65 plus) will exceed that of children (0-14 years). The following table gives the ratio of the elderly to 100 children, in a number of countries.

Country	*2000*	*2030 (projected)*
Italy	127	261
Japan	115	231
Greece	114	206
Bulgaria	106	244
Germany	103	187
USA	59	102
China	27	91
India	14	38

Today, it is most important that we ask ourselves where are the problems coming from and therefore, what strategies and approaches we need to adopt to shift the current flows of policy, program design which will transform us.

The 3 important issues raised by Devki Jain are:-

1. To shift our perception to the marginalized female elderly.
2. To shift or change our negotiating instruments, our basis and methods of advocacy.
3. To identify ourselves with a specific national platform.

I do not hesitate in saying that we, action-oriented people, often feel that action is more important than thought.

However, an idea is really more powerful. Gandhi ji, when he picked up a fistful of salt on the beaches, it was not the symbolic gesture came from the masses and with the idea of fist full of salt...came civil disobedience.

So, the first idea that I suggest we have to see is the single poor senior women, not as helpless creatures who need our benefaction, but as agents of change, as economic and political actors.

These elderly women and their knowledge of survival must be considered for the design of the programme that we want to bring forward.

I quote Amartya Sen

"We need a vision of mankind not a patient whose interests have to be looked after, but as agents who can do effective things — both individually and jointly. We also have to go beyond that role of human beings specifically as 'consumers' or as 'people with need' and consider, more broadly, their general role as agents of change who can — given the opportunity — think, assess, evaluate, resolve, inspire, agitate and through these means, reshape the world."

I believe that women's knowledge which comes out of their lived experience, generates the best ideas not only for their own rehabilitation, but for resetting the political economy towards economic and social justice.

As it stands now the voices of elderly women are marginalized and it is now only "a women tent".

Hence, Devki's suggestion is that we move ourselves to negotiating our ideas, our knowledge into the public domain, knowing amongst ourselves that it emerges from our lived experience.

We could talk about:-

- Preventing and reducing the burden of disabilities, chronic diseases and premature mortality.
- Reducing the risk factors associated with non-communicable diseases and functional decline and individual's age, while increasing factors that protect health.
- Enacting policies and strategies that provide a continuum of care for people with chronic illness and disabilities.
- Providing training and education for formal and informal careers.
- Ensuring the protection, safety and dignity of ageing individuals.
- Enabling people, as they age to maintain their contributions to economic development, to activities in the formal and informal sectors, and to their communities and families.

There are many theories on how the construction of knowledge by women is not only different from men, but is built upon collective experience, built upon inclusion, built upon lived experience.

Identify with some platforms, it has been well recorded that women engage in collective action with greater ease and occurrence than men. One of the examples is, the remarkable pension strike and togetherness of women by

Aruna Roy recently, where thousands of women gathered under the banner of Mazdoor Sangh and has demanded higher pensions for elderly widows. In Kerala, a remarkable transformation has taken place, the status of women has been brought about by Kudumbshree, which has become a deep collective voice of women of Kerala.

In other words, we have to now shift our voices to generate ideas and engage in public debates.

During my nationwide deliberations, as the chairman of the review committee of National Policy of Older Persons constituted by Hon'ble Minister, I have experienced the pain and trauma of the elderly. I am now fully convinced that we need a mechanism like department of Welfare for Elderly, a National Commission for the elderly so as to better understand and resolve this concern towards financial, healthcare, shelter, welfare and other needs. It is my experience that the elderly cannot go to hundred different departments for their pensions, healthcare and other needs. We need a one widow clearance and protection for older women against abuse and exploitation.

Let us call in our own respective places, be an instrument of change by mobilizing, advocating, pressurizing, agitating and working for the health care of elderly.

I am confident that the government of India would soon put into action the various recommendations made by the NPOP Review Committee on Ageing.

9

Micro Pension Literacy Programmes and Pension Savings

Dr. Kavim V. Bhatnagar

1. Backdrop to Demographic Changes and Issue of Old Age Income Insecurity

A majority of India's informal sector working poor, especially low income women workers in urban and rural India, are highly vulnerable to old age poverty since, they are not only excluded from any formal pension provisions, but also unable to access any regulated insurance and retirement savings product at an affordable transaction cost. Empirical evidence suggests that while there is limited existence for 'risk of life' (life insurance), coverage of 'risk of longevity' (pension) is mostly unheard of. With 17 years of life expectancy at 60, workers will need to accumulate enough savings during their working life to support themselves for nearly 15 - 20 years, when they are too old to work. However, their fragile labour market attachments and modest intermittent incomes, coupled with the absence of a low cost and easily accessible long-term savings mechanism and above all, the concept of pension, so conspicuously missing, puts retirement planning out of reach of most of these workers. This presents a bleak outlook for the next generation of India's elderly and clearly suggests that old age poverty will continue to be an intractable public policy challenge. For a majority of these low income workers, and equally for the States and Central Government therefore, a vital issue is the management of the longevity risk with the cessation of earnings in old age.

With 320 million senior citizens by 2050, India might be heading for a socio-economic demographic catastrophe, if the younger population fails to create pension saving today. Striking demographic changes have occurred during the previous and current century, with the increase in the number and proportion of elderly in the Indian population. With the improvement in healthcare industry and life expectancy, however, the elderly are also experiencing more of the cumulative effects of multiple chronic diseases and disability, leading to increased expenses in the old age. The growing needs of the aged population require the availability of more caretakers and money at their disposal and commitment to geriatric care. Yet, numerous reports have documented a widespread insensitive or negative attitude held by the younger cohorts toward aging and the care of the elderly. Such biases may, in part, be due to the general societal attitude towards the aged and they may further reflect the traditional non-orientation of beliefs, customs and sanskaram, which emphasizes the care and management of older generation by the younger cohorts. Financial constraints in the old age and similar crunch of resources amongst their children, add fuel to the fire.

Providing opportunities to the working poor to build up savings for retirement through thrift and self-help, is an important public policy goal. Yet, barely 5% of this group is presently saving for retirement and less than one in five, have some form of insurance.[2] Even for this cohort which is actively saving for their old age, the savings accumulations are as modest as an average savings corpus of those above

45 years at Rs.25,000 or less.[3] Hence, the best case scenario, even for those presently saving for their old age, is that they will manage enough pre-retirement savings to support themselves for no more than two years, when they decide to stop working or are unable to work.

Traditionally, the Indra Gandhi National Old Age Pension Scheme (IGNOAPS) has been the primary public policy intervention for India's destitute elderly.[4] At present, 169 lakh persons above the age of 65 years, living below poverty line, are receiving central assistance under IGNOAPS. The revised[5] norms, effective 1st April, 2011 of lowering the age limit would benefit about an additional 72.32 lakh persons in the age group of 60-64 years, who are living below the poverty line. It is estimated that 26.49 lakh persons above the age of 80 years and living below the poverty line, would become eligible to receive enhanced central assistance at the rate of Rs. 500 per month. However, as the population of elderly is estimated to grow from the present 90 million to 200 million in the next two decades, the cost of a meaningful tax-funded old age pension, may be unsustainable for future governments. Future governments however, may be unable to escape the fiscal burden of the elderly, as nearly half of India's low income workers expect some financial support from the Government in their old age. The continued growth in nuclear households and the growing incapacity of low income joint and extended households to support non-earning elderly, will further intensify this pressure.

2. 'Need' and 'Demand' for Pension Products amongst the Low Income Workers

The Evidence from the Indian Retirement, Incomes and Savings Survey, 2005 of the Ministry of Finance and the Invest India Incomes and Savings Survey, 2007 suggests that a significant proportion of India's working poor are willing and capable of saving for their old age. But to achieve an above poverty pension, they need supplementary savings from the government along with a secure environment where their modest savings are channeled to customized long term savings products and earn high real returns at a low transactions cost.

Nearly a third of India's low income workforce believe they will need to work well into their old age, as they would be unable to accumulate enough savings to otherwise support themselves.[6] Most, however (nearly 60%), have given no thought to their retirement income needs, including more than half of those over 40 years old for whom old age income security should be a front-of-mind issue. Importantly, more than 90 percent of the working poor who expect to be unable to work beyond a certain age, are making no active preparations to support themselves in their old age. Motivating this cohort to start saving for their old ages through a Individual Retirement Accounts (IRA) under a regulated mechanism, is a daunting task in India for the public policy protagonists.

Three pillars of inclusive growth namely, Creation of economic opportunities through generation of full and productive employment; Broadening economic opportunities through capability enhancement and ensuring minimum well-being by providing social protection to the vulnerable and the needy, can easily be served by means of deferred income in the form of pension. It could be achieved by providing opportunities to the working poor to build up savings for retirement through thrift and self- help, as an important public policy goal.

Interestingly, while there could be a huge latent 'Need' for pension amongst the low income informal sector workers, there is no or little 'Demand' for such products, as the concept of 'Pension for Poor' is absent in India. Pension at best, is considered a prerogative of few civil servants and employees covered and eligible under the 'Employees Pension Scheme' of the EPFO. Thus, pension literacy plays a predominant role in transforming a 'latent need' into a 'demand'.

Two strategies for converting need into demand are identified. One, a longer term programme that involves raising the level of 'want', or perceived need, through attitude change. The other has a more immediate impact and involves increasing the rate at which perceived needs are converted into demands by reducing organizational barriers. It is argued that, potentially, a quarter of the adult population is susceptible to demand expansion under the second strategy. Although racial and social class differentials in perceived need would be unaffected by such a programme, inequality in demand would be reduced. A number of quite specific initiatives are suggested. First, the retentiveness of the pension system as a need for social and economic security in old age, can be increased, especially among marginal groups, through the establishment of a more egalitarian partner relationship, by the exercise of human relationship skills, through behavioural strategies for increasing compliance and through improved access. Secondly, improved geographical access can be achieved through tapping the 'captive' populations present in two major institutional areas, the SHGs and farmers club or Cooperatives. This requires mobility in deployment of resources and flexibility in negotiating the organization and financing of care. It is only once the 'need' for pension in the old age is established that one finds that people start owning the scheme. By owning the scheme one finds that people start contributing on a regular basis and not just on an initial one. Finally, more rational visit schedules, organizational arrangements and payment systems, need to be developed in the average contribution practice.

Invest India Micro Pension Services[7] is a specialized agency, that is imparting pension literacy in India, using its various service delivery partners to deliver the same with an eye on enrolling members in the Micro Pension. It creates awareness amongst women on issues of old age income insecurity and inculcates amongst them the concept of importance of long- term savings for retirement. It also offers them a platform where these women actually join Micro Pension and save as little as Rs. 200.00 pm on a monthly basis, into their individual retirement account (IRA) with their full contributions reaching the fund manager namely, UTI Retirement Benefit Pension Fund (UTI RBPF) at the backend. It is a Government of India notified pension scheme, at easy and affordable cost to the working poor, with 80% of its customers being women belonging to SHGs, JLGs or cooperatives, etc.

3. Pension Literacy: Goals, Means and Challenges

Need assessment is perhaps the foremost goal and precursor of creating awareness on old-age income insecurity. It is a shift towards a more customer-focused approach, where design is not the shiny layer around a crappy product, but a new way of thinking. In the traditional approach to market research, one would ask statistically-average people to respond to a survey that asks them, what they want. But Henry Ford already noticed that consumers are not able to express themselves properly when he remarked *"If I'd asked my customers what they wanted, they'd have said a faster horse"*. That's why these techniques rarely come up with any important insights and are only useful for pointing towards incremental innovation. They will never come up with those ground-breaking, paradigm-shifting, game-changing breakthroughs that make us think '*why didn't anyone think of that before?*'

While the tools used for creating awareness on old age income insecurity may range from game play to spring cartons (expressing income and expenditure gap), the techniques used are time- tested like generative sessions. The technique of generative sessions is particularly used to create interests amongst the participants. The initial discussions get focused on creating awareness on' old age issues' rather than savings pattern. A set of questions that the members answer, do well for the members to start thinking on lines of issues that they might face when they become old. Answers to the set of questions are very well known to the group, but the group had never ever considered them as significant to think as they might have tried to avert such uncomfortable thinking on their own. The session is targeted against the group to realize that, they would become old after a certain period, and would find a dwindling income to meet an inflating basket of commodities and services to buy. They also appreciate the fact that the short- term mismatch in their income and expenses, when they are young are catered to by the local MFIs, bank credit, money lenders or even friends and relatives. But, none of these agencies would ever come forward to provide a helping hand in their old age and the doors for credit, whether from MFIs or banks, would be permanently closed, once they cross a certain age. This realization, using the generative and interacting session, usually come to the members on their own rather than being imposed upon them so that, there is an inner realization that would travel a long way in becoming a Micro Pension member.

First, we need to put the customer at the heart of the organisation. Our sole purpose is to add value to his or her life. Secondly, we should get out of the office and talk to real customers. And thirdly, we should find ways to truly understand their behaviour, because behaviour is never right or wrong, they are always meaningful experiences. Capturing these experiences allow us to gain a deep understanding of their needs and motivations.

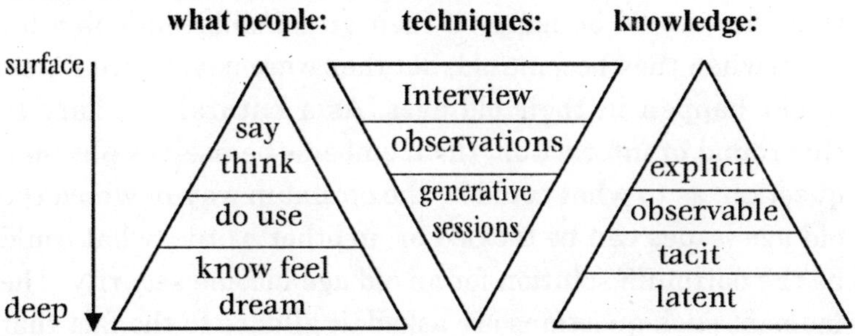

If one takes a look at the different levels of knowledge, one sees that traditional market research focuses on the things customers say or think; explicit knowledge. But to gain a deeper understanding, one should observe one's customers behaviour. Then, one finds that there are so many more things they are not able to express, simply because they are not aware they are doing things that were not intended that way. And, there are techniques to gain an even deeper understanding of customer behaviour. Generative techniques help people to articulate the latent needs, they may not even know they have. Tools like context mapping, deep psychological research, cultural probes and maketools, enable customers to reflect on their own experience in order to become aware of their experiences.

Once the need is established, the solutions are also discussed in a participatory manner where, the moderator or trainer facilitates a discussion on the probable solutions to the issue. This may range from considering options like the intergenerational subsidy where the elder generation looks after the younger generation socially and the reverse is performed on an economic platform, to government assistance in the form of social security pension. Members on their own respond to such facilitation and conclude that neither the government, nor the panchayats would ever look after them in their old ages. However, they always opine that they would be happy if their grand/children look after them when they become old, but they were never sure if that might happen in their old ages. As a natural corollary to this round of interaction, the members themselves put up a question, as to what could be the optimum way in which the old age issues can be tackled or, in other words, what could be the optimum solution for an old age income security. The moment such questions are asked, it alludes to the fact that now the 'need' is getting converted into 'demand'. At this stage, one would do well to talk about the broad features of a Micro Pension scheme. This includes objectives, features, benefits and risks and returns associated with Micro Pension as a product. All critical features that have a bearing on their decision making are discussed with them in a participatory manner. One of the star attraction amongst such discussions is the 'magical power of compounding' also known as 'time value of money' in financial parlance. They are also explicitly apprised about the risks of investment in a market oriented product such as a mutual fund, that has a balanced portfolio and the NAV based variable rate of return, very similar to a typically bank return that varies from year to year on its TDR.

Typical IEC material in local language designed after substantial research is extensively used in the most interactive manner, to keep the interest of the members alive. A lot of research has gone into designing and imparting such material in a uniform manner across various languages, using local traditions. It may include, but is not limited to, interactive generative sessions, stories, flip chart and various tools, etc. Since, this is neither a typically enrolled classroom delivery of literacy, nor a sales pitch for Micro Pension, it has to be very carefully imparted using the local channel partners such as NGOs and MFIs that are working at the grassroot level.

Once the members realize the importance of old age income in/security, the optimum way to deal with such a situation is to give them time, enough to contemplate over the need. They are then asked to go back to their homes and discuss these issues with their spouses and family members and identify, if at all they need such a product for their old age as Micro Pension. The risk here is that one fourth / third of such members, who attended the literacy and awareness campaign might opt out and decline to join the scheme. However, the flip side is that the rest who would now join Micro Pensions, would join it only after they have a complete understanding of the product and process and would be a long-time permanent loyal investors to the Micro Pension.

Micro Pensions	
Year 2006 marked the beginning of a Micro Pension movement where 25,000 low-income young women workers like vegetable vendors, rag pickers, canteen runners et al of Sewa Bank in Ahm-edabad pledged to start saving for their old age. For thousands of years, the women of India had to	Fair, Safe, Secure, Sustainable mechanism of old age savings. Tailored to the Needs of the Working Poor with low amount of savings and flexibility in contributions. Secure, Scalable and Low- Cost Approach that does not allow middlemen or agencies to impact on savings.

work until the last day of their lives and, had been the bed-rock of the family structure of India. Today, the move-ment has percolated into more than 70 districts of India across nine states with reputed Micro Finance Institutions, Non - Gover-nment Organisations, Coo-peratives etc, facilitated by pension and development sector experts focussed on enabling and assisting India's rural and urban more than 2,00,000 working poor to achieve a dignified retirement by thrift and self-help through a unique and proprietary Micro-Pension TM model.	National Coverage and Impact in over 18 states with more than 150 districts using the reputed MFIs, NGOs cooperatives and Bank channels. Reaching the working poor through SHGs and RRBs. Targeted Delivery of Government Co-contributions as in case of Rajasthan and other states. Administration and Extensive Use of IT in order to maintain centralised record-keeping and individual accounting. Customised and Regulated Pension and Insurance Products providing high real returns.

Pension literacy comes with its own challenges, ranging from poor literacy levels to extremely poor understanding on financial literacy, like budgeting and financial planning. It is difficult to explain about savings for a long-term product such as pension to a client who typically start earning at dawn, start spending in the forenoon, spend by the afternoon, fail to even see their monies by the dusk and never saves for tomorrow. The challenge is to motivate them to save for the day, day after tomorrow or years together. Next is the financial position of a lot many clients who understand the concept of old age insecurity and are also willing to save, but have no surpluses to do so. To such members one would do well to quote examples of non- essential expenditure like quitting a cup of tea and a pair of beedi daily could save them a Rs. 7.00 a day contributing to Rs. 200.00 a month. Stories like Ganga -Jamuna, the twins who start pension savings at different ages and get different outcomes, explain the concept of 'start early' amongst the members. Most of the members of the SGHs are found to be saving savvy, but have no concept of savings for a long- term or pensions. It has been found that even after the members understand the importance of Micro Pensions, and join the scheme, some are found to be quickly dropping out for various reasons. Thus, the challenge is not in getting the members to sign up for Micro Pension, but the greater challenge is, to continuously keep them motivated so that they contribute into their individual retirement account of Micro Pension, month after month on a sustainable manner. One of the biggest foes of financial savings for the long- term is 'Inflation' as, it eats up a major chunk of pension savings over a long period. Thus, the concept of inflation, price rise and diminishing value of money with time, are a few financial concepts that have to be told to the group in their own languages. Members are also encouraged to raise their contribution level year after year, to meet the challenges of rising price and inflation, so that the value of their pension corpus may also keep pace with the inflation, so much so, that the returns from the portfolio are more positive real (more than inflation).

The following chart depicts the probabilistic numbers in case of regular savings under certain assumptions of rate of contributions and return. However, the picture is clear under the assumption that an average 30 years old women who could save Rs. 6.50 - Rs. 7.00 a day only by means of savings through a 'Tea and Beedi', example as mentioned above, can earn a corpus (assuming a 10% CAGR) of approximately Rs. 3,60,000 by the time she is 58 years old. This can produce for her (assuming 10% return), a monthly income stream of Rs. 3000.00, without the corpus being eaten up. Hence, an amount of Rs. 3000 pm for self, same amount for spouse after the death of the pensioner and a corpus of wealth created for above Rs. 3.5 lakh for the next generation, can be earned only by means of Tea and Beedi. Not a bad bargain at all, provided it is communicated well and they adopt the same.

Value of Corpus and Subsequent Monthly Pension for Members Joining at Various Age

Member's Age at Time of Joining	*No. of Years of Contribution*	*Total Contributions*	*Value of Member's Contributions at Retirement*	*Life Long Monthly Pension with Corpus Paid Back*
18	40	96000	1264816	10540
20	38	91200	1032068	8601
25	33	79200	617866	5149
30	28	67200	366119	3051
35	23	55200	213110	1776
40	18	43200	120113	1001
45	13	31200	63590	530
50	8	19200	29236	244
53	5	12000	15487	129

Assumptions:

1. Amount of monthly contribution: Rs. 200.00.

2. Rate of Return earned by corpus during accumulation (up to 58 years of age) phase: 10%.
3. Rate of Return earned by corpus during distribution (after 58 years of age) phase :10%.
4. Rate of Withdrawal after 58: Only 10% of return from corpus.
5. Corpus is never withdrawn and only return from the corpus is paid as pension.

Note:

- The numbers mentioned are only indicative and depict the power of compounding and bear no resemblance on returns out of any pension or mutual fund.
- The chart does not assure any guaranteed returns from any investment.

Finally, to conclude the discussion, the fact is that India's economic growth and demographic transition is resulting in a falling birth rate, a slowing down of the death rate and is fast resulting in sharp rise[8] of the proportion of the aged population. A large part of the informal sector remains without any funded social security scheme. What further complicates the matter is that only about 10-12% of the working population participates and is eligible to participate in the mandatory, formal programme designed for providing income security during the non-earning years. These employees are largely part of the formal sector (private sector and the government). The rest is either part of the informal sector (which goes unreported in the broader economic scheme) or does not enjoy adequate income streams that can be accommodated in the existing pension schemes.

Women in particular, are perhaps the worst affected. With frequent breaks in their working age due to child birth and rearing, coupled with a higher life expectancy at retirement age of 60, but little or no savings, exposes their vulnerability to old age income insecurity. By the time they realize that they ought to have saved for their old ages, they have already missed the bus.

Unless awareness is created amongst them, in their own language and manner using participatory approach, it would be difficult to convince them by an externally forced agent. Hence, pension literacy is ought to be treated more as a participatory discussion making the target audience realize what they knew already, but has always been on the back of their mind rather than explicitly coming out naturally. The literacy is only targeted against, breaking the dormancy of thinking over the issues that we all are aware of, but never dared to contemplate upon. As a consequence, more than 90 percent of the working poor, are making no active preparations to support themselves in their old age. While this is largely due to low financial literacy, almost 1/3rd of these workers expect their children to support them when they are no longer able to work. However, given the probability of their children, also being in the low income workforce, this strategy is tenuous at best. India still has a young population and unlike our western counterparts where the baby boomers have started retiring with little or no balances in their pension accounts, we have the opportunity to save for a decent retirement, if only we wake up ourselves in time.

References

1. Micro Pension® is the registered trademark of Invest India Micro Pension Services.

2. Invest India Income and Savings Survey, 2007.
3. Analysis from the Report titled "Towards a Financially Inclusive Financial System: Financial Services Demand and Utilisation by India's Low Income Workforce" produced by IIMS Dataworks with NABARD, SADHAN, ISMW and IIMPS in 2008 an based on the Invest India Income and Savings Savings Survey 2007 produced by IIEF and IIMS Dataworks.
4. A tax funded old age pension for below Poverty Line elderly aged 65 and above. Government of Inida transfers a subsidy of Rs. 200 per such elderly per month to State Governments who in turn add Rs. 200 on an average to this subsidy. Each State Government is responsible for delivery of this subsidy of Rs. 400 per month to the eligible aged population.
5. Recently in June 2011, the Cabinent has approved lowering the age limit for the Indira Gandhi National Old Age Pensions Scheme (IGNOAPS) from 65 years to 60 years and at the same time increased the rate of pension from Rs. 200 to Rs. 500 to persons of 80 years and above.
6. Analysis from the Report titled "Towards a Financially Inclusive Financial System: Financial Services Demand and Utilisation by India's Low Income Workforce" produced by IIMS Dataworks with NABARD, SADHAN, ISMW and IIMPS in 2008 and based on the Invest India Incomes and Savings Survey 2007 produced by IIEF and IIMS Dataworks.
7. Promoted (2006) by organizations like Sewa Bank, UTI, Dell Foundation et all IIMPS strives to provide a dignified retirement to the working poor. It provides a low cost, secure, scalable and transparent mechanism to the working poor to save for their old age. IIMPS is delivering regulated pension products and services to more than 200,000 working poor in collaboration with MFis, cooperatives, worker unions, government departments, Banks and its BCs and AMCs in eighteen States. IIMPS has developed a unique Micro Pensions™ model that delivers individual pensions and insurance accounts to the poor and also links its pan India partnership network. Using this model, millions of low income workers with modest savings and located anywhere in India can access retirement and insurance products. IIMPS also undertakes a range of developmental, promotional and educational initiatives

to motivate mass scale coverage of contributory pensions by the working poor.

The proportion of those aged 60 and above is expected to climb from 4.6% in 2000 to 9% in 2030. In absolute numbers, the number of people above the age of 60 will increase from 87.5 million in 2005 to 100.8 million in 2010 and this is expected to jump to 200 million by 2030. By 2050, it is expected to be over 320 million. (*Source* — World Population Ageing: 1950-2050, United Nations).

10

Science and Technology for Ageing Population

Prof. P.N. Tandon

The inevitability of ageing and death has preoccupied humanity for more than 5000 years, which also effected prince - Siddhartha (later Lord Buddha) in India and the Sumerian King of Uruk. The ancient medical system - Ayurveda, devoted a whole separate section on ageing and how 'Rasayana' can rejuvenate the aged. It is not just a matter of statistics, of chronological aged versus the young, but the real issues will be to determine Disability—Free life expectancy or disability—Adjusted ageing as highlighted by Sanderson and Scherbor (Science 2010).

To provide for successful, healthy ageing is a complex issue with its social, psychological, economic, emotional and medical components intertwined with each other. However, from a scientific, including medical perspective it is necessary to determine factors contributing to—

(*i*) Increasing healthy life span.

(*ii*) Preventing diseases, adversely affecting achieving long life.

(*iii*) Understanding how ageing predisposes to pathologies.

(*iv*) To prevent / provide relief from physical and psychological debilities associated with ageing.

(*v*) To improvise and utilise technologies to compensate for age-related disabilities.

Before considering these it is important to identify problems specific to India:

1. More than 70% of those ≥ 60 yrs. live in rural areas.
2. Large population living in tribal and remote areas.
3. More than 70% people are employed in unorganised sector have no security of pension.
4. Absence of comprehensive social security.
5. High prevalence of poverty / illiteracy.
6. Feminization / Widowhood problems.
7. Double burden of diseases still prevalent.
8. Health Insurance not possible for those above 65 yrs.
9. Labour force Migration.
   (i) Internal ----------Rural to Urban.
   (ii) External ----------to other countries.
10. Lack of old people homes / domiciliary support system.
11. Lack of specialised health care services for the elderly.
12. Inadequate teaching / training in Geriatrics.
13. Rising cost of health care.

The last decade has seen many remarkable developments in the field of biology of ageing - the emerging field of Biogerontology. It primarily has two goals:

(a) An understanding of the ageing process itself, since the fundamental mechanisms of ageing remain uncertain.

(b) To improve the health of older people through understanding of the biological mechanisms that underlie pathology. (Phil. Transc. R.Soc. Jan 2011)

Biogerontology

The "new science of ageing" is directed towards two goals, (i) an intellectual one i.e. the understating of the ageing process, and (ii) to improve the health of older people. Despite all the recent advances, the fundamental mechanisms of ageing remain uncertain. A dominant idea within this field is the stochastic accumulation of damage to biomolecules which is a major driver of ageing, while the processes that reduce levels of such damage promote longevity. But, this is still an hypothesis and not a proven fact. (David Gems : Phil. Trans. R. So. 13, 366, 108-112, 2011)

Current research on the biology of ageing, suggests that there is a reasonable possibility that treatments that decelerate human ageing can be developed and this in turn can minimise the risk of age-related pathologies. The important question is whether biomedical interventions can postpone ageing (particularly healthy ageing). The overarching question is not whether mean human life span will increase modestly over the next decades. It almost certainly will, assuming continued success in reducing old-age morbidity and mortality. The goal of human ageing research is not necessarily to extend life span, but instead to extend the healthy years of life and add life to years.

Extending Healthy Life Span – From Yeast to Human

Ageing is a complex process of accumulation of molecular, cellular and organ damage, leading to loss of function and increased vulnerability to disease and death. Minimizing these damages will not only prolong life but, will extend healthy life span. (Fontana et al Science 328, 321, 2010)

According to Andrzej Bartke, the mechanism that probably underlies the extension of both life span and health span of these animals includes increased stress resistance, improved antioxidant defences, alterations in insulin signalling. A shift from pro to anti-inflammatory profile of circulating adipokines, reduced mammalian target to rapamycin mediated (TOR) translation and altered mitochondrial function, including greater utilization of lipids when compared to carbohydrates.

In terms of treatment for ageing, three different goals of biogerontlogy are:

- Compressed morbidity
- Arrested ageing
- Decelerated ageing

The important questions that biologists have attempted to answer are:

(a) Can Ageing be Delayed / Slowed Down/ Postponed

There is a vast amount of data, both from animal experimentation and human studies that provide unequivocal evidence that ageing can be delayed, postponed or slowed down. The two major factors influencing this are (i) Genetic, and (ii) Environmental.

Genetics

Ageing and longevity appear to be determined by a complex interplay of the genetic endowment with environmental influences [Finch and Tanzi, Science 1997, 278, 407-411]

Heritability studies comparing the concordance of life-span in monozygous and dizygous twins estimated a 25-30%, genetic contribution to human life span varialious. (Hjelmberg et al 2006, Hum. Genet. 119, 312-21). There are a large number of studies in different parts of the World which support this hypothesis.

- Leiden Longevity Study.
- Ashkenazi Jewish Centenarian Study.
- Danish 1905 Cohort Study.
- Iceland Study.
- The Baltimore Longitudinal Study.
- Italian In CHIANTI Study.

While it needs to be reiterated that life span is the outcome of complicated processes that might involve thousands of genes and non-genetic factors, a number of studies point to the importance of two specific genes i.e. FOXO3A and APOE. Aubrey de Grey - British Biologist who believes that with the advances made in biotechnology it will soon be possible to rewrite genetic code, so as to reverse the ageing process.

Environmental Factors

The few environmental factors that have been shown to the associated with extreme survival are avoidance of smoking and severe obesity and relatively high educational attainment. In addition, psychological factors are important.

Dietary Restriction

As early as 1930 it was observed that rodents subjected to dietary restriction increased their life-span. This has since been confirmed in other species including human as well.

(Bishop, Lu and Yanker : Nature 464, 529, 2010)

Calorie restriction has also been widely documented to have beneficial effects on the functions of the brain and its vulnerability to age dependent pathology, reduced age-related atrophy in rhesus macaques, has significant beneficial effects on age-dependent impairment of learning and memory in rodents and humans. Unexpectedly - a three verbal memory by approx 20% (Witte et el PNAS 106, 1255, 2009)

In rodents, both dietary restriction and decreased nutrient sensing pathway activity can lower the incidence of age-related loss of function and disease, including tumors and neurodegeneration. Dietary restriction also increases life span and protects against diabetes, cancer and CVD in rhesus monkeys and in humans it causes changes that protect against these age related pathologies. (Fontana et al: Science 328, 321, 2010)

In humans, dietary restriction provide major and sustained beneficial effects against obesity, insulin resistance, inflammation, oxidative stress and left ventricular diastolic dysfunction. (Fontana and Klein 2007, Fontana et al 2004)

(b) Can Ageing be made Healthier

Although, the ageing process was originally viewed as a time of decline of physical and cognitive functions, the concept of successful ageing, put forward by Rowe and Kahn in 1987, triggered a large interest in the study of biological, psychological and psycho-social determinants of successful ageing. In 1987, Rowe and Kahn described successful ageing as having three main components:

- avoidance of disease disability
- maintenance of cognitive capacity
- active engagement in life

Across various spheres of science, positive attitude towards ageing have been shown to positively influence memory performance, longevity, health, well being, life satisfaction, will-to-live and other physiological and psychological functioning (Levy 2000).

A McArthur Foundation Longitudinal Study of successful ageing led to the following conclusions:

- Low levels of education were associated with poor psychological function, poorer health behaviour and biological conditions.
- Some psychological, psychosocial and physiological variables predicted cognitive decline later in life.
- A low number of social ties at the time of entry into the study predicted cognitive decline 7 yrs. later.
- Elevated levels of IL 6 were significant predictor of cognitive decline 2.6 yrs. later.

At the policy level, the support provided by the Govt. to promote joint family, would pay rich dividends.

Levy et al (2001) in their observational study showed a 7.5 years mean survival advantage for those who expressed a more positive self - perception of ageing compared to those who hold more negative perception.

(c) Can Disease related to Ageing be prevented

Many of the diseases commonly associated with ageing like hypertension, cardio-vascular disease, stroke, metabolic syndrome, cancer etc. can be prevented by following a sensible life style. Voluminous literature is available on the subject which need not be elaborated here. The role of obesity in pathogenesis of these diseases is well known. Similarly, the damaging effect of tobacco consumption in any form – smoking or chewing, is well established. The beneficial effects of exercise and variety of meditation practices for physical and mental health is scientifically proven. Utilising this knowledge, it should be possible to lead a healthy life which in turn results in healthy ageing.

This is yet another, till recently, unrecognised pathogenesis mechanism which predisposes to some of the diseases associated with ageing. (DJP Barker : J. Int. Med. 216, 412-417, 2007)

A variety of epidemiological studies in diverse geographical areas led to the hypothesis that undernutrition in utero and during infancy, permanently changes the body structure, physiology and metabolism and leads to coronary heart disease and stroke in adult life. It is therefore, logical to accept that preventing under-nutrition in utero and infancy will provide healthier and longer life.

One of the common, often accepted as inevitable, consequences of ageing is cognitive decline. This has been a subject of a large number of scientific studies. A number of psycho-social and biological measures including some chemical and herbal drugs and even a vaccine are under various stages of clinical trial.

(d) What are the Technological Inputs to Maximise Function (Implants, Transplants, Bionics, Robotics, Electronic Sponsors etc.)

Help is available in the form of a large number of artifacts which maximise or replace age related functional impairments. Hardly an aged individual goes through life without these, be it the age old artificial denture, hearing aid, optical glasses, or the more sophisticated implants and transplants like cardiac pacemakers, deep brain stimulators and other bionic and robotic devices. To these may be added the whole range of organ transplants and currently under trial stem cell based therapies. The primary purpose of all these is to add life to years and not just add years to life. (Tandon 2006).

Conclusions

There is unmistakeable evidence that we, like many other developed countries in the world, are going to face the psycho-social, economic, biological and medical problems of the inevitable large number of aged people in our country in near future. Notwithstanding the formulation of a Policy for the Aged by the Government of India nearly a decade ago, it is obvious that as of today the country is ill-prepared to meet these challenges. While this would require committed efforts by social scientists, economists, policy makers and executives, help can also come from scientists – biogerontologists to come together in evolving research strategies and program planning to ensure a healthy, happy and economically sound ageing population.

11

Social Protection, the Informal Economy and Older Women

Ratna M. Sudarshan

1. Context

The term 'social protection' and the debates and discussions for whom, and how – have gained momentum since the mid – nineties. Internationally, greater attention began to be given to social protection after the experience of the Asian financial crisis, which resulted in a huge loss of jobs, and as more evidence came in to suggest that globalisation and its economic and financial repercussions have adverse consequences for certain groups and sectors. The national context within which the contemporary discourse on social protection is situated, has been set by changes in the macro policy framework and internal pressures for labour market reform on the one hand and continuing evidence of high levels of poverty and vulnerability on the other.

It is possible to see that the early 80's mark a watershed in both the economic policy framework and the thinking on social protection in India, although while some of the linkages between these two are explicit, others are implicit and not always easily visible. Prior to 1980, the policy approach and programmes that could be included under the rubric of 'social protection' were narrowly defined and the outreach was very limited. Post 1980, the discourse in this area is marked by efforts to expand both concept and outreach, although the actual achievements may fall short of the intentions. The change in the thinking regarding social protection, owes much to the concerns that a higher growth rate of the economy will be difficult to sustain over time without, also simultaneously improving the productivity of workers, conditions of work, and fall- back positions/safety nets.

Both, in relation to concept and outreach, the main challenge to social protection policies and programmes has come from the existence of a huge informal economy, the overlap between informality and poverty, and thus between 'social protection' and 'poverty eradication'. The often divergent concerns of those primarily focused on growth, and those seeking to ensure the rights of workers, have found common ground in the contestations over social security.

2. Defining Social Protection

The idea that governments have a responsibility to initiate public action, to ameliorate the poverty and vulnerability of individual citizens of a country, is an old one, yet it is only in the last decade that 'social protection' has emerged as an important component of development planning in Asian countries. The more commonly used terms in the past have been social security and social assistance; others that are used are social welfare and social insurance. These terms include within them the concept of 'protection' but in different ways. Perhaps, the most specific and clearly defined of these terms is 'social security'.

Social security was defined by the ILO in 1989 as follows:

> "The protection which society provides for its members, through a series of public measures, against the economic and social distress that otherwise would be caused by the stoppage or substantial reduction in earnings resulting from sickness, maternity, employment injury, unemployment, invalidity, old age and death; the provision of medical care, and the provisions of subsidy for families with children".

The 'core contingencies' that ought to be covered by social security, according to the ILO, are thus as identified above. Implicit in this definition is the view that the normal status of a person is to be employed, and the role of social security is to provide help in coping with injury, sickness, etc., as listed above. The ILO has contributed substantially to developing and expanding the concept of social protection, including the need to extend security to all workers (not just those in the organized sector). It has also sought to highlight the potential of linking social protection to local economic development (Rodriguez-Pose 2001). More recently, the definitions used by the ILO have expanded the concept substantially to include notions of universality and rights (Reynaud 2002).

Social security continues to be linked with the idea of workers contributing something towards times of need, and receiving a parallel contribution from the state. But, the more typical situation in developing countries is one where people work, but do not earn enough to cover their basic needs - the 'working poor'.

The term **'Social protection'** is used in a broader sense than social security. A broad definition has been given by Devereux and Sabates Wheeler (2004):

"SOCIAL PROTECTION is the set of all initiatives, both formal and informal, that provide: social assistance to extremely poor individuals and households; social services to groups who need special care or would otherwise be denied access to basic services; social insurance to protect people against the risks and consequences of livelihood shocks; and social equity to protect people against social risks such as discrimination or abuse".

The four main elements of their framework are:

- **Protective measures** that provide relief from deprivation, such as narrowly targeted safety nets for people facing livelihood shocks (e.g. food aid as emergency relief) and, social assistance for the chronically poor (e.g. disability benefit, social pensions).
- **Preventive measures** that seek to avert deprivation, including formal social insurance schemes (e.g. health insurance, unemployment benefits); informal risk-pooling mechanisms (e.g. savings clubs, burial societies); and diversification strategies to spread risk.
- **Promotive measures** that aim to enhance incomes and capabilities, while remaining grounded in social protection objectives (e.g. school feeding or public works, which transfer food or cash to smooth short-term consumption and also promote long-term asset formation).
- **Transformative measures** that seek to address vulnerabilities arising from social inequity and exclusion (e.g. collective action for workers' rights, protecting minority ethnic groups against discrimination, or sensitisation campaigns on HIV and AIDS).

(Devereux and Sabates - Wheeler 2004; IDS In Focus 2006)

This definition reflects an understanding that social protection seeks to deal both with absolute deprivation as well as with risk and vulnerability. Sources of vulnerability include illness, maternity, asset loss, disability, unemployment, old age, death - but, also poverty and social exclusion. It includes public action, and 'all initiatives, formal and informal'.

An approach to social protection that has served to sharpen the thinking around the concept is the World Bank's **Social Risk Management Framework**. This framework sees the basic need for social protection, in the fact that people are vulnerable to shocks of various kinds - anticipated, unanticipated, individual, covariant, and so on. There are different ways of enabling people to cope with these situations, and a distinction can be made between:

- Risk aversion or the avoidance of risk, preventing occurrence
- Risk mitigation or reducing the impact
- Risk coping or managing the effects

Thus, social protection is linked to the contingencies that affect people. In this framework, it is difficult to extend the concept to include basic needs or chronic deprivation.

Kannan, has argued the need for social protection to encompass both-Basic Social Security and Contingent Social Security, with Basic Social Security referring to the need to meet 'deficiency' in such basic wants as food, health, education and housing, and Contingent Social Security-the need to meet 'adversity' such as sickness, accidents, old age (Kannan 2004).

Even though social protection is generally understood as a responsibility of the state, researchers have suggested that the role of community based security may at times be most crucial, as the state provided schemes are often less easily accessible (Home Net South East Asia 2006).

Other terms that have been more widely used in the past include social assistance and social insurance, which identifies a particular type of public action to deal with aspects of vulnerability. **Social assistance** refers to transfers made by the state to those with no other means (or inadequate means) of coping, and these have historically evolved from 'charity' to 'rights'. These are tax based and based upon legal rights, but subject to specified conditions under which they can be paid out. **Social insurance** refers to contributory schemes for anticipated contingencies (including pensions, medical benefits). The right to any benefit is acquired by making a contribution. (Subrahmanya 2000: 38-40).

It is important to note that the definition of social protection is itself an evolving one, responding to new empirical observations as much as conceptual ones.

3. Social Protection Approaches in India

Despite all the effort to evolve a universally applicable definition, context remains important to interpretation. In the context of developing countries, social protection continues to be closely linked to development planning and policy. In India, social protection is being defined in a very different context from that of developed countries: demographically, this is a young country (over 30 % of the Indian population is under the age of 15); and the 'norms' of social protection have to be defined against a context of prevalent poverty. Economically, the organized sector has remained a very small part of the total economy (over 90% of the workforce continues to be in the informal economy).

The initial introduction of social security schemes in India was heavily influenced by the Western understanding of the concept at that time. Social security was thus linked to employment in the organized sector; the expectation at

Independence, being that with development the organized sector would grow to provide employment to the majority of workers, as is the case in the developed countries. Today, however, as more concerted effort is under way to define appropriate social provision and initiate universal programmes, the contextual differences become increasingly more significant in assessing what is the best way forward.

The basic decisions to be taken in implementing a programme of social protection, include deciding :

(a) should the programme be targeted to a particular group or universal;

(b) should it be contributory, tax based, market determined, or community based.

In India, social security is mandated by Article 32 of the Constitution, and supports the idea of universal coverage for specified situations:

> "The State shall, within the limit of its economic capacity and development, make effective provision for securing the right to work, to education, and public assistance in case of unemployment, old age, sickness, disablement and other cases of undeserved want."

A two-pronged approach was taken in implementing this mandate, through the provision of 'social security' on one hand and 'social welfare' on the other. Social security was designed for workers employed on a regular basis in the organised sector. It included an employees' insurance scheme, and a provident fund scheme. The coverage of the schemes has been gradually expanded over the years. Social welfare was seen as a set of interventions to assist the destitute, classified in the first Plan as categories of women, children, youth, family, SC, ST, other backward classes, the physically handicapped and others.

Both sets of programmes cover a small group of persons – social security being available to workers in the organized sector and social welfare to a percentage of those in extraordinary difficulties and without other means of support.

For workers in the unorganized sector, the main approach has been the setting up of sector specific Welfare Funds (usually tripartite in nature). Welfare funds include contributory and tax based schemes. Tax based schemes have been set up by the Government of India for beedi workers, mine workers, cine workers and construction workers. A cess is levied on the production or export of goods. Through the funds, workers have access to medical care, education of children, and other specified forms of assistance. The Government of Kerala has set up several contributory welfare funds, for different groups of workers. Contributory schemes have been assessed as having lower coverage and, it is often difficult to get all the contributions. So, from this point of view tax based schemes may be seen as better. Most expenditures from welfare funds have been to cover health, education and housing expenditures and in that sense, are not available for the conventional social security benefits such as maternity, invalidity, occupational injury, etc. The actual range of benefits varies considerably across the funds. The beedi fund requires that a worker has an identity card that often has to be issued by the employers. Without this card, benefits cannot be claimed. As a result, coverage of the fund is limited and probably only 50-60 % of the workers have cards. Despite problems, the welfare funds have been an important way of reaching out to unorganized workers (Subrahmanya 2000: 67)

Other relevant state initiatives include, provisions of labour laws for social security; social insurance; micro credit; NASP (maternity, old age, health); PDS and food security; housing; basic income through public works; welfare funds.

While labour laws may not be seen strictly as 'social protection', in so far as they have a direct bearing on the conditions of work and the benefits to which workers have access, they do influence the overall assessment of levels of protection available in the society. Social insurance seems very much a product of the post- 1980 period, in fact largely post- 1990. This is also true of micro credit and the National Social Assistance Programme which seeks to cover maternity, old age and health. While the Public Distribution System is one of the oldest initiatives, the more targeted interventions (mid day meals for all primary school children, and the targeted PDS) are post - 2000. Housing schemes have also been started post 1980. Wage employment programmes too have a long history, but nothing as ambitious as the NREGA has been attempted earlier. Similarly, an explicit focus on trying to develop programmes for informal workers is seen in the 1990's, especially, in State level welfare funds (as in Kerala and in West Bengal). Although, the largest welfare fund (for beedi, workers) was set up earlier, the expansion to other workers has mainly been in the 1990s.

The current outreach of government social protection is limited, and the report of the National Commission on Enterprises in the Unorganised Sector on Social Security estimates that only 5-6 % of workers are covered by existing schemes (NCEUS 2006). This means that in practice, people cope with contingencies and chronic problems by relying upon traditional mechanisms of support, including borrowing from neighbours, contractors, employers and relatives. The NCEUS proposed, an Unorganised Workers Social Security Bill provides a national minimum social security: health benefits (including health insurance, sickness allowance and maternity benefits), life insurance and old age benefits, as a contributory scheme with worker, employer and government each paying Re 1/ day/ worker, with the Central Government making the payment on behalf of workers below the poverty line.

The well being of a person depends both on resources within the individual's control, and on the environment within which one lives. Examples to illustrate this point range from clean air and safe drinking water, to availability of natural resources, and access to health and education facilities. However, this 'collective' aspect of social protection has found less emphasis is the mainstream discourse.

The approach that any country takes to social protection can be expected to be a function of its ideology and its macro economic policy framework. If macro policy favours the free market, social protection is likely to take the form of mechanisms which can also be handled through the market. Where there is reliance upon a high degree of state intervention and public ownership, social protection approaches can be expected to favour subsidies of various kinds, public provision, and so on. In economies that are in the process of opening up and liberalizing their economies, we may expect to find changing forms of social protection too.

Apart from market determined forms of social insurance, some innovative programmes have been started by non-government organisations, for example, SEWA's health package.

4. The Age Factor

How have age and gender been reflected in the approach to social protection?

Pension payments are a clear focus on the elderly, that is, those who are no longer able to work. Although, the original understanding of 'pensions' is linked to the idea of a 'working age' and then an age of 'retirement' - concepts relevant to those in regular full-time organised sector employment - there is an understanding that some basic income transfer to all elderly persons is an obligation of the state. Second, a programme like the NREGA does not make age a criterion of exclusion, neither does it seek to design work suited to bodily ability.

The idea of 'substantive equality' is useful in trying to assess the gender sensitivity of social protection. This concept suggests that the circumstances in which people are placed needs to be taken into account, and further that equality requires looking at impact and the context and reality of disadvantage. Substantive equality allows for special measures to be taken, so as to provide a level playing field and address the inequalities and disadvantages of context.[2] A review of social protection measures in India shows that the 'context' of women's lives is reflected in the provisions for maternity leave. For all other measures, women and men are treated on par, i.e. there is a formal equality in the treatment of men and women among those groups who get covered (organized sector workers and some groups of unorganized workers). The approach taken to ensure outreach of social security to women as, well as men has taken the form of providing quotas for women, as in the wage employment programmes. Women's reproductive role is recognised through the provision for maternity benefits and nutritional support to pregnant and nursing mothers. The provision of quotas, is some recognition that formal equality will not lead to equal outcomes without special measures. At best, it can be said that some efforts has been made for accommodating and including women in the system of social protection, as designed. The design, itself is largely based on the identified needs of workers in formal employment and on the international codes.

'Older women' or senior citizens may be so defined, from the age of 58 or 60 years upwards (although these definitions vary from one purpose to another). The table below tries to summarise the key sources of vulnerability for older women.

Table 1: Older Women: Sources of Vulnerability

	'young old' – able to work (linked to physical fitness rather than age!)	*'Older Old' — unable to work*	*Role of state*	*Role of family, comm-unity*
Liveli-hood	Informal workers continue to work and need all the support any worker needs: conditions of work, secure wages, enough work. But bodily ability changes and hence, nature of work an issue	Wholly dependent on pensions (or family, community support)	Permitting the elderly to work is not enough; need to review nature of the work to be done by the old Pensions linked only to age	
Health	Includes both loss of bodily strength and illnesses. Marital status/ gender differentiated	Loss of mob-ility, vision	Access to medi-cal care: ensure services irres-pective of abi-lity to pay Information	Commun-ity and voluntary effort emo-tional support and pra-ctical ass-istance Indigenous knowle-dge and practi-ces.

Food	Access to basic rations	Lower intake and may need special supplem-ents	Access to rations - + affordable special supplements	
Housing	Assured shelter	Assured shelter as well as care giver	Support to volunteers/ care givers for the elde-rly; training information.	

5. Looking Ahead

This very preliminary attempt, to look at the role of social protection in the lives of elderly women, suggests a few areas where more thinking and practical efforts are needed.

First, crossing a certain age is linked to the growing vulnerabilities in health, ability to work, and loss of independence. As the economy strengthens its overall social protection efforts, these need to be nuanced to take note of the age factor. Thus, while NREGA is to be complimented for not making age a bar to participation, the next step is to see that if the scheme is being accessed by the elderly. Can we design suitable work under the scheme ? Or can we substitute a simple cash transfer, if no suitable work can be found ?

Second, what happens to us with age, depends greatly on how we were placed when we were young. Do we have savings? Do we have children who are earning well and are willing to support us? Do we have strong social networks and community support? Do we live in our own homes and with easily accessible medical care? Clearly, the experience of age, while similar in many respects, is also differentiated by economic well being and social situation. In a dominantly poor country, the focus of state effort needs to be on the poorest, while also being sensitive to the needs of all elderly people.

Third, while state support is essential, there is an enormous role to be played in educating and spreading awareness about old age problems, and ways to deal with them, so that families and communities are better informed. Similarly, useful traditional practices and indigenous wisdom need to be better understood and recognized.

Fourth, gender leads to additional concerns in aging, since health issues are gender differentiated, more women live without spouses, and social norms continue to put them in weak positions within the family and community.

And finally, this is a good time to attempt gender and age sensitivity within the social protection approaches in India, given both the prevalent optimism on the overall economic performance front and the stronger political support for social protection, than in previous decades.

References

1. Devereux, Stephen and Rachel Sabates-Wheeler, (2004), 'Transformative social protection', IDS Working Paper 232 at http://www.ids.ac.uk/ids/bookshop/wp/wp232.pdf.
2. Home Net South East Asia. 2006. Social Protection for Home Based Workers in Thailand and the Philippines.
3. IDS In Focus May 2006.
4. Kannan, K.P. 2004. Social Security, Poverty reduction and Development: Arguments for enlarging the concept and coverage of social security in a globalizing world. ESS Paper No 21. ILO, Geneva.
5. NCEUS. 2006. Report on Social Security for Unorganised Workers. At http://nceus.gov.in/

6. Reynaud, Emmanuel. 2002. The extension of social security coverage: the approach of the ILO. ESS Paper No 3. ILO, Geneva.
7. Rodriguez-Pose, Andres. 2001. The role of the ILO in implementing local economic development strategies in a globalized world.
8. Subrahmanya, R.K.A. 2000. 'Strategies for protective social security', 'Support for the unorganized sector: existing social security measures' and 'Welfare Funds' in Jhabvala, Renana and R.K.A. Subrahmanya (ed) The Unorganized Sector: Work Security and Social Protection, New Delhi: Sage. pp. 38-73.

12

Welfare of the Armed Forces Aged

Gautam Sen

Every year, nearly 60000 Armed Forces officers and personnel-below-officer rank, retire or get discharged from active service. The retirement takes place at different ages, as per the rank of the officers and other personnel, going out of service. Unlike their Civilian counterparts, the Services retirees and those discharged, are less aged and may not strictly be classified as senior citizens in the 60+ age group. A large number of these persons, are therefore capable of rendering productive service to the nation for a good number of years, after they leave the Defence Services. It is therefore, in the national interest and also for their welfare that these persons be effectively harnessed in different spheres of the country's socio-economic activity.

The Director General of Resettlement (DGR) functioning under Ministry of Defence (MOD) : Secretary (Ex-Servicemen Welfare) (ESW), is intended to perform the role of a facilitator in regard to placement of the Services's retirees and discharged personnel, in different civil organisations, within and outside the govt. The Directorate, headed by a serving Major General or equivalent, and having a mix of Service and Civilian officers and employees below- officer-category, has therefore an onerous role to perform in relation to the above-stated activity.

Placement in the civil domain is not an easy task. The retired or discharged personnel have to have the requisite skills and professional abilities, to be acceptable to the civil organisations and perform the professional role expected of them. While discipline and commitment are their manifestly discernible traits, some special efforts or attuning by way of training and counselling are necessary for these personnel, particularly in the last 2-3 years of their service, in trades and professional attributes of jobs available and suited for them in the civil market. Civil-employment-oriented training under the aegis of DGR, is however, being imparted on a systematic basis, and on an average, more than 30000 serving personnel including officers, are trained annually and nearly 2000 personnel trained after they have already left the Services.

Department of (ESW) MOD, was set up in September, 2004, with the objective of helping in the resettlement of ex-Servicemen and their proper placement in civil society. Dept. of ESW's role extends beyond resettlement and placement activities, and encompasses the provision of healthcare through the Ex-Servicemen's Contributory Health Scheme (ECHS) (*headed by a Major General rank Service Officer as MD*) as well as assisting in the resolution of ex-Servicemen's pension-related grievances. The spread of these activities is quite substantial considering that there are nearly 20 lakh ex-Service men, with a huge segment aged over 60+ years, and more than 3 lakh widows. Though, the total number of placements achieved is not very large, it is not insignificant either. As per records of MOD : Dept. of ESW, during the period 2001-2005, a total of only 46000 (i.e. approx. 10000 annually) ex-Servicemen JCOs/ORs found placements in the govt., private and security sectors taken together. This figure has increased bymore than 4 times by 2010-11. The arrangements for healthcare through ECHS have also been expanding and the outlay of 2011-12 is Rs. 1028 crores. Therefore, from the organisational arrangements put in place, it is evident that the Central Govt. is conscious of the need for comprehensive action towards welfare of our Service personnel, post-discharge-cum-retirement.

While focus of action and concomitant responsibility in respect of welfare of ex-Servicemen has been retained with MOD and its attached organisations, i.e., DGR, MD: ECHS and Director : Kendriya Sainik Board (KSB) through their budgets and welfare programmes, it is nevertheless necessary to maintain a strong linkage with the various macro social sector schemes of Govt. of India. This is notwithstanding that, many of the schemes of Govt. of India are basically oriented to the marginalised sections of society, the rural and urban poor and below-poverty-line populace. The Union Govt. Civil Ministries and Departments could set aside a portion of their budgets, in an institutionalised manner, and devise modalities in consultation with MOD, for gainfully engaging the Services retirees and discharged personnel in civil jobs, albeit with age relaxation and for specified years, as well as promoting the welfare of these persons and their dependants within the ambit of the civil sector Central schemes. Planning Commission of India may be involved to work out the modalities albeit in consultations with MOD, with a holistic approach. The new concept of common fund-base for all schemes without distinction of Plan-Non-Plan (as per recommendations of the Rangarajan Committee on efficient financial management), would facilitate matters, and the present arrangement where under every transaction or scheme directly or indirectly associated with Defence, has perforce to be accommodated under Non-Plan budget allocation - and, there was always a fund constraint under Non-Plan with Govt. of India, would be done away with.

The Confederation of Indian Industries (CII) and the various Chambers of Commerce, can play a vital part towards harnessing the inherent abilities of our retired/discharged and retiring Service officers and lower rank personnel, their productive capacities and thereby, enhancing their welfare after they leave service with the Defence Forces . The thrust of efforts for finding placements, could be centred on the technical, and particularly regimental personnel like those belonging to the Corps of Electrical and Mechanical Engineers, Corps of Signals and Corps of Engineers, who have professional skills which can be easily utilised in the civil sector. To cite an example, Lt. General (Retd.) Shamsher Mehta, who had served as Deputy Chief of Army Staff (dealing with weapons' modernisation) and also our Western Army Commander ; as a nodal officer at CII, had worked effectively for promotion of such placement activity and synergy between the industry and governmental Defence production effort. The Army Medical Corps doctors and paramedics have however been doing well to fend for themselves. After retirement or discharge, a large number of them have, on their own, found jobs in civil hospitals and premier medical organisations. However, some of them have gone to the other extreme of trying to prematurely quit the Service, after they have acquired professional expertise through training, service secondments, etc. at govt. expense, without rendering mandatory service in the Defence establishments. Such cases fortunately, do not form the majority of those leaving the AMC.

On the whole, post-retirement or discharge, the Services, personnel including officers, are better placed vis-à-vis their Civilian counterparts. However, the issues of concern in terms of welfare of families of Service personnel, particularly of below- officer- rank, relate to widows and children of those who expired or wives and children of persons who had to leave service prematurely owing to disablement or injury consequent on operations directly or incidentally. Apart from taking care of the financial needs of such families, there is a need to ameliorate their trauma and rehabilitate them in a manner that they feel that society wants them to contribute to national development and welfare. The Services, through their regimental (non-governmental/in-house) funds, are quite active in this regard. Notwithstanding this involvement, reinforcing efforts by banking and non-banking financial institutions as well as constructive NGOs, are concomitantly needed. In respect of the aged widows and destitute children of personnel affected as above, as well as those family members of similarly affected service personnel, who have come of age and are suffering from physical or mental debilities the Service officers' wives associations are playing an ameliorating role. This is a well-meaning effort but limited in scope. Though the Rajya Sainik Boards (RSBs) have stepped into this role, their involvement of the RSBs as well as civil society groups, would be helpful if organised in a structured manner under the aegis of MOD : Dept. of ESW as well through the apex body - the KSB.

Our Defence Forces officers and their subordinates are unique in all respects during service and are in a position to play a contributory and catalytic role in India's development and stability. Their welfare when out of the Services and when they come of age, cannot be ignored. Institutions are available but adequate synergy in their functioning is needed. Govt. of India has been very positive in this respect and supportive action by all the State Govts.is necessary. The Central Govt. has recently enhanced the funding of activities of RSBs to 60% - for Special Category States (North Eastern States, Sikkim, Uttarakhand, Himachal Pradesh and Jammu and Kashmir) (the remaining portion is to be funded by the respective State Govts.), as against 50% share of the Central Govt. earlier. Rs. 35 crores was targeted to be released in 2011-12. Governors and Chief Ministers of the States statutorily serve as Chairmen and Vice-Chairmen, respectively of the RSBs with retired Service Officers functioning as Secretaries of the Boards. Therefore, the RSBs, which are basically an interface between the Central and State Scheme implementing authorities and the ex-Servicemen and families/dependants, have adequate authority and expertise and should be effective facilitators of the ex-Servicemen's welfare. The RSBs could henceforth, move from an overseeing to a more executional role vis-à-vis the development schemes flowing from the Central and State Plans. Institutions created should thrive and serve the target groups with proper end-result.

13

National Programme for Health Care of the Elderly: An Initiative towards Active and Healthy Ageing in India

Dr. Damodar Bachani

Preamble

The unprecedented increase in human longevity in 20th century, has resulted in the phenomenon of population ageing all over the world. Countries with large population such as India, have large number of people aged 60 years and above. The population over the age of 60 years, has tripled in the last 50 years in India and will relentlessly increase in the near future. In 2001, the proportion of older people was 6.9% which will increase to 8.2% in 2011 and 9.2% in 2016.

According to the 2001 Census, there were 75.93 million Indians above the age of sixty years; of them, 38.22 million were males and 37.71 million were females. The projections for the next five Censuses till the year 2051 are: 96.30 million (2011), 133.32 million (2021), 178.59 (2031), 236.01 million (2041) and 300.96 million (2051).

Along with rising numbers, the expectancy of life at birth is also consistently increasing, indicating that a large number of people are likely to live longer than before. The expectancy of life at birth during 1996-2001 was 62.3 years for males and 63.39 years for females. The projected data for the periods 2001-2006, 2006-2011 and 2011-2016 are 63.87, 65.8 and 67.3 for males and 66.1, 68.1 and 69.6 years for females.

Non-communicable diseases requiring large quantum of health and social care, are extremely common in old age, irrespective of socio-economic status. Disabilities resulting from these non-communicable diseases, are very frequent which affect functionality compromising the ability to pursue the activities of daily living. The treatment/management of these chronic diseases is also costly, especially for cancer treatment, joint replacements, heart surgery, neurosurgical procedures, etc., thereby making it out of bound for the elderly whose income decreases post retirement and more so, for the elderly in the unorganized sector and dependent elderly women.

The National Sample Surveys of 1986-87, 1995-1996, and 2004 have shown that:

- The burden of morbidity in old age is enormous.
- Non-communicable diseases (life- style related and degenerative) are extremely common in older people, irrespective of socio-economic status.
- Disabilities are very frequent which affect the functionality in old age, compromising the ability to pursue the activities of daily living.

The National Sample Survey of 2004 (60th Round), provides a comprehensive status report on older persons. According to it, the prevalence and incidence of diseases as well as hospitalization rates are much higher in older people than the total population. It also reported that about 8% of older Indians were confined to their home or bed. The proportion of such immobile or home bound people rose with age to 27%, after the age of 80 years. Women were more frequently affected than males in both, villages and cities. The survey estimated the state of self- perceived health status of older people. A good or fair condition of health was reported by 55-63% of people with a sickness, and 77-78% of people without one. In contrast, about 13-17% of surveyed population without any sickness, reported ill health. It is possible that many older people take ill health in their stride as a part of "usual/normal ageing". This observation has a lot of significance, as self- perceived health status is an important indicator of health service utilization and compliance to treatment interventions.

A multi-centric study observed the following burden of various diseases in the elderly in India:

Health Problems in elderly	*Rural*	*Urban*
Poor Vision	47.3	43.3
Bowel complaints	31.4	31.8
Hypertension	31.8	44.7
Anemia	19.8	13.8
Difficulty in Hearing	21.6	19.4
Arthritis	37.4	34.7
Diabetes	9.8	16.9
Depression	25.5	21.6
Urinary/Constipation	19.6	12.0
Weight Loss	23	16.2
Asthma	7.8	5.4
Fall/Fracture	9.3	8.2
COPD	5.9	3.6
TB	3.7	2.5
IHD	7.0	8.3

Very little effort has been made to develop a model of health and social care, in tune with the changing need and time. The developed world has evolved many models for elderly care e.g. nursing home care, health insurance, etc. As no such model for older people exists in India, as well as most other societies with similar socio-economic situation, it may be an opportunity for innovation in health system development, though it is a major challenge. The requirements for health care of the elderly, are also different for our country. India still has family as the primary care giver to the elderly and scope for training this lot, provide support to the programme. Presently, the elderly are provided health care by the general health care delivery system in the country. At the primary care level, the infrastructure is grossly deficient. The elderly suffer from multiple and chronic diseases. They need long-term and constant care. Their health problems also need specialist care from various disciplines e.g. ophthalmology, orthopedics, psychiatry, cardiology, dental, urology, to name a few. Thus, a model of care providing comprehensive health services to the elderly, at all levels of health care delivery, is imperative to meet the growing health needs of the elderly. Moreover, the immobile and disabled elderly need care, close to their homes.

National Programme for Health Care of the Elderly

The National Programme for the Health Care of the Elderly (NPHCE) is an articulation of the international and national commitments of the Government, as envisaged under the UN Convention on the Rights of Persons with Disabilities (UNCRPD), National Policy on Older Persons (NPOP) adopted by the Government of India in 1999 and Section 20 of "The Maintenance and Welfare of Parents and Senior Citizens Act, 2007" dealing with provisions for medical care of Senior Citizens.

The program was initiated in the year 2010-11 with the following vision:

- To provide accessible, affordable, and high-quality long-term, comprehensive and dedicated care services to an Ageing population.
- Creating a new "architecture" for Ageing.
- To build a framework to create an enabling environment for ***"a Society for all Ages"***.
- To promote the concept of *Active and Healthy Ageing.*
- Convergence with National Rural Health Mission, AYUSH and other line departments like Ministry of Social Justice and Empowerment.

Following are the specific objectives of the programme:

- To provide an easy access to promotional, preventive, curative and rehabilitative services to the elderly through community based primary health care approach.
- To identify health problems in the elderly and provide appropriate health interventions in the community with a strong referral back-up support.
- To build capacity of the medical and paramedical professionals as well as the care-takers within the family, for providing health care to the elderly.
- To provide referral services to the elderly patients through district hospitals and regional medical institutions.

To achieve these objectives, following strategies have been evolved:

- Community based primary health care approach including domiciliary visits by trained health care workers.

- Dedicated services at PHC/CHC level including provision of machinery, equipment, training, additional human resources (CHC), IEC, etc.
- Dedicated facilities at District Hospital with 10 - bedded wards, additional human resources, machinery and equipment, consumables and drugs, training and IEC.
- Strengthening of 8 Regional Medical Institutes to provide dedicated tertiary level medical facilities for the elderly, introducing PG courses in Geriatric Medicine, and in-service training of health personnel at all levels.
- Information, Education and Communication (IEC) using mass media, folk media and other communication channels, to reach out to the target community.
- Continuous monitoring and independent evaluation of the Program and research in Geriatrics and implementation of NPHCE.

A multi-tier service delivery system will be established as per the following framework:

Health Facility	Packages of services
Sub-centre	• Health Education related to healthy ageing. • Domiciliary visits for attention and care to home bound / bed ridden elderly persons and provide training to the family care providers. • Arrange for suitable callipers and supportive devices from the PHC to the elderly disabled persons to make them ambulatory. • Linkage with other support groups and day-care centres operational in the area.

Primary Health Centre	• Weekly geriatric clinic run by a trained medical officer. • Maintain record of the elderly using standard format during their first visit. • Conducting a routine health assessment of the elderly persons based on simple clinical examination relating to eye, BP, blood sugar, etc. • Provision of medicines and proper advice on chronic ailments. • Public awareness on promotional, preventive and rehabilitative aspects of geriatrics during health and village sanitation day/camps. • Referral for diseases needing further investigation and treatment, to Community Health Centre or the District Hospital as per need.
Community Health Centre	• First Referral Unit (FRU) for the elderly from PHCs and below. • Geriatric Clinic for the elderly persons twice a week. • Rehabilitation Unit for physiotherapy and counselling. • Domiciliary visits by the rehabili-tation workers for bed-ridden elderly and counselling of the family members on their home-based care. • Health promotion and prevention. • Referral of difficult cases to District Hospital/higher health care facility.

District Hospital	• Geriatric Clinic for regular dedicated OPD services to the elderly. • Facilities for laboratory investigations for diagnosis and provision of medicines for geriatric medical and health problems. • Ten-bedded Geriatric Ward for in-patient care of the elderly. • Existing specialities like General Medicine; Orthopaedics, Ophthalmology; ENT services, etc. will provide services needed by elderly patients. • Provide services for the elderly patients referred by the CHCs/PHCs, etc. • Conducting camps for Geriatric Services in PHCs/CHCs and other sites. • Referral services for severe cases to tertiary level hospitals.
Regional Geriatric Centre	• Geriatric Clinic (Specialized OPD for the Elderly). • 30-bedded Geriatric Ward for in-patient care and dedicated beds for the elderly patients in the various specialities viz. Surgery, Orthopaedics, Psychiatry, Urology, Ophthalmology, Neurology, etc. • Laboratory investigation required for the elderly; special sample collection in OPD.

- Tertiary health care to referred cases from med. colleges, district hospitals and below.

Present Status

At present, the program is being implemented in 100 districts across 21 states of India. District hospitals are being strengthened for management of the elderly. Health professionals are being trained in problems in the elderly and home based care of the bed-ridden cases. All districts will have 10 bedded Geriatric Ward and a Geriatric OPD on a daily basis, for care of the elderly. The Government of India provides assistance for the following components:

- 10-bedded Geriatric Ward and a Geriatric OPD.
- Drugs and consumables, machinery and rehabilitative appliances.
- Transport of referred/serious patients.
- Home based care for bed- ridden cases.
- Additional human resources (Consultant Medicines- 2, Nurses-6, Physiotherapist-1, Hospital Attendants- 2 and Sanitary Attendants-2).
- Training of health professionals.
- IEC activities.
- Operational Costs.

Geriatric clinic are also being set up at Community Health Centers. A Rehabilitation Worker is being recruited for physiotherapy and medical rehabilitation services for the elderly. CHC are also supported with certain appliances and aids for the elderly. Domiciliary visits will be undertaken for the bed-ridden elderly and counselling to family members for care of such patients by the rehabilitation workers. Support is also being provided for transport of referral cases, IEC activities, consumables, etc.

At the Primary Health Centers, the Medical Officer will be in-charge for coordination, implementation and promoting health care of the elderly. A weekly geriatric clinic will be arranged at PHC level by trained Medical Officer. Support will be given with certain appliances and aids for the elderly. Home based care will be for the bed- ridden cases. Support is also being provided for transport of referral cases, IEC activities, consumables, etc. Female and Male Health Workers posted at sub-centres, will be trained for health care of the elderly. Annual check-up of all the elderly at village level, need to be organized by PHC/CHC. Certain appliances and aids required for the elderly, will be provisioned at sub-centres.

Eight Regional Geriatric Centers have been supported with provision of 30 geriatric beds, training and research and starting MD in Geriatric Medicine.

Future Plan

During the 12th Five Year Plan (2012-2017), the program is proposed to be expanded to cover all districts of the country in a phased manner. It is also proposed to develop 12 additional Regional Geriatric Centers in selected Medical Colleges of the country. These centers will provide tertiary level care for referred cases, undertake training and research in the field of Geriatrics. The proposal also includes establishment of National Institutes of Ageing (two) in the country.

Following are the expected outcomes of these efforts in the coming years:

- 20 institutions with capacity to produce 40 postgraduates, MD in Geriatric Medicine per year.
- Additional 6400 beds in District Hospitals and 800 beds in Medical Colleges for the elderly.

- Geriatric Clinics in the OPD and Physiotherapy units in 640 District Hospitals and more than 2000 Geriatric clinics in CHCs/PHCs.
- Free aids and appliances to elderly population.
- Improvement in life expectancy and better quality of life of the elderly population.

14

Moving Towards Self Reliance: Pension and Security for the Elderly

Rani S. Nair

"In the end it is not the years in your life that count; it is the life in your years" (Abraham Lincoln).

Every milestone in a human being's life is looked forward with anticipation and joy - whether it is the birth of a child, the first day in school, the first job, marriage et al. The only event that is dreaded, avoided or inappropriate for discussion is 'retirement' and 'old age'. The majority do not look forward to retirement and old age with anticipation because it is felt that this cycle of life is synonymous with decline in productivity, economic insufficiency and social irrelevance.

With industrialization and urbanization, the aged had become a forgotten generation, as they were neither economically relevant nor socially prominent. The aged were expected to live out the post-retirement years in the shadow of their family. For the aged, life was always in sepia tints, never Technicolor. Today, this scenario has changed. With increasing longevity, better healthcare and more opportunities, the 60+ population aspires to live an economically and socially productive life.

With the change in demographic profile, changing social structure and low pension coverage in developing countries, the focus on old-age income security has intensified. In the past, old-age income security was inbuilt in the fabric of social and religious custom. The concept of the affluent providing for the disadvantaged, especially the old and infirm through charitable donations and religious endowments was widely prevalent. Families and communities joined together to provide and care for their old. As a result, the old were not left to either depend upon their personal resources or on their own capacity to earn in their old age. The concept of savings - whether in the form of house, land, gold, jewellery, etc. - was also a means of providing economic power to the old. Lure of inheritance ensured old age income security and better care from the younger generation.

Today, the acquisition of assets is not within the means of most people, due to inflationary pressures. The high cost of living and the high cost of health care tend to erode the savings of the older generation. With increasing longevity, the post-work period is equal to the productive period. Consequently, relatively better-off citizens too are outliving their savings or facing a resource crunch. For the marginal workers, old age income security is solely their capacity to work.

The issues which affect old age universally, are: (i) access to good health care, and (ii) adequacy of income to pay for basic services like food, housing, water, electricity, etc. In developing countries, older people, who are not covered by adequate social security, find it difficult to access basic health care and necessities like water electricity, housing, etc. Rapid urbanization has led to the alienation of the old people, either alone in the villages or in large cities. Globalization, change in family values, increasing pressure on the earning family members to provide for the needs of the aged as well as the young, has resulted in neglect of the elderly. Today, many older people are suffering in silence. We need to hear their voices, to make them speak out so that the younger generation, who are still economically productive, will learn from their experiences.

Pensions are a means of reducing the poverty of the elderly, as they ensure a direct cash transfer to the aged population. Countries and agencies, like UN and the World Bank, are trying to push the agenda for social protection by making it a global initiative. Today, more than 80 countries have put in place social pensions, which may be either contributory or non-contributory, aimed at providing regular cash transfers to older people. The emphasis on old age income security has intensified as the number of the aged increased. By 2050, majority of the elderly will be living in developing countries. The issue, facing the world, is not longevity but the quality of life of the elderly. Helpage publications have indicated that while almost 1 in 10 people is over the age of 60 today, by the year 2050, almost 1 in 5 people in developing countries, will be over the age of 60. By the year 2050, India and China will have a large population of old and the people aged over 60 will outnumber children aged 0 -14 years.

India is conscious that unless pension coverage is extended to the unorganized sector, the ageing of the present work-force will add to the fiscal stress on the budgetary resources. Efforts are already under way to provide for the elderly through the National Social Assistance Programme (NSAP) wherein one of the components is provision of pension. The eligibility criterion is that the age of the applicant (male or female) should be 65 years or above and the person should belong to a household living below poverty line (BPL family) as per the prescribed Government of India's norms.

In spite of the several initiatives undertaken by the Government towards social security, pension coverage in India remains low as compared to many countries as can be seen below:

Country	Pension coverage
OECD	70% of working age population
East Asia	18% of working population
South Asia	7.5% of working population
India	10 -15% of older people

Source: Pensions at a Glance: Asia/Pacific, OECD/World Bank Report.

While the organized sector has provision for pension, the unorganized sector is out of the social security net as per the chart below:

Segment	% of pension coverage
State/Central Govt. employees	2.8
EPFO/Other formal PF Arrangements	10.0
Uncovered (Unorganized)	87.2

The majority of the population of India, is in the unorganized sector. Further, as more women work in the unorganized sector, there is a gender bias to ageing and absence of pension coverage. The National Commission for Enterprises in the Unorganized Sector (NCEUS) based on National Sample Survey Organization (NSSO) 55th Round 1999-2000 data have estimated that out of total 396.76 million workers in India, 362.8 million i.e. 91.3% are engaged in informal employment including the informal workers in organized sector. Social security and designing of pension products, becomes important in the Indian context.

As we look at old-age income security, we have to look at it with the twin perspective of ensuring that:

(i) the population of this country which is aged 50 + years is able to retire with dignity, and

(ii) the population aged 25-50 is covered by designing pension products that will enable Indians to retire comfortably.

Since the 50 + population do not have the advantage of productive years to its benefit, there is an immediate need to address issues of old-age income security. For the financially secure, generous tax exemptions to encourage pension saving during the remaining productive years could be one such option. For others with limited saving capacity, state support as in the case of Swavalamban Yojana of Government of India and similar co-contribution scheme by some State Governments encourage, self-reliance through utilizing small savings to build an adequate corpus. For the needy aged poor, old age pension schemes could continue as a means of support financed by the Budget. In the immediate term, there is need for a means tested pension coverage moving to universal coverage in the long term.

The designing of a pension product for the 25-50 age group, who have decades of economically-productive life, is the second challenge. There is need to encourage the young working adult to start saving for old age from the moment of obtaining employment. The NPS, launched by the Government of India, envisages that through a voluntary pension system people with a defined contribution can make their old age secure. In order to popularize NPS, the Government has launched the Swavalamban Yojana, wherein from the financial year 2010-11, if any person, from the unorganized sector, contributes between Rs. 1000 - Rs. 12000 per annum towards his pension, the Government would make a co-contribution of Rs. 1000 per year for five years. The endeavor of the Government through the Swavalamban Yojana has been to ensure that a minimum pension of Rs. 1000 per annum should be made available under NPS.

While the NPS is open to all citizens of India, special emphasis has been given to the small investors through NPS-Lite. Through the aggregators' model, institutions of the Central Government, State Government, self-help groups, micro-finance institutions, etc., who are engaged in the business of providing socio-economic services to the poorer sections of society, could be engaged to provide pension coverage to large sections of marginal workers in the unorganized sector. The NPS Lite/Swavalamban was launched in September, 2010 and in the short period of 6 months; more than 3 lakh subscribers have joined the scheme. Swavalamban, through NPS-Lite, has started a new movement to provide a platform for secure investment and income security in old age.

Pension is just one aspect of providing for old-age security. It provides economic power to the aged. However, there is need for a fundamental shift in policy and opinion-making, on the role of the aged in society. There is need to reassess the real economic and social contributions of the elders in society. There is a need to re-think the role of society in helping elderly retain their independence. Older people are not passive. They contribute to their families and to community in different ways. But their contributions are minimized and often under-valued by a society geared to economic success only. In every family, older women and men provide help - in farming, in trading, in child-care, in domestic work, etc. Older people also contribute to the well-being of the house-hold and family; provide a sense of continuity both in the family and in the community.

But the lack of economic resources trivializes their contribution to family and society. There is a need, as longevity increases to:

(i) Provide a pension or annuity to ensure a steady monthly income. There is need also to sustain the elderly in part-time work, etc. Engagement in less physically-strenuous tasks would provide them with not only an income, but also mental and physical agility and well-being.

(ii) Support the older people in being physically fit, with access to healthcare. Raising the quality and coverage of basic health-care would minimize the impact, of illness and disability for the older people.

(iii) Build society around the family and community, especially, as industrialization and globalization lead to migration of people from their homes to cities in search of work. Traditional family values are disappearing as societies become more and more materialistic. As families and societies are strengthened, such support systems would provide support to the old and the infirm. There is a need to re-emphasize and re-affirm the traditional family values of love, respect and tolerance towards the elders in society.

(iv) Address the safety issues which is another is of concern in old age security. Support can be provided for the aged in the form of Self Help Groups. Such groups would provide a social network for the older members to rely upon. The key should be to enable older people to mutually support themselves and remain independent as long as possible.

Creating solidarity through a network, providing access to health-care, providing means for extending the working age and providing an annuity or pension for the sunset years, would all contribute to make a difference in the lives of the old. As societies grey, we need to build the necessary social infrastructure as a means of support for an ageing population. Society needs to convert its elderly into its opportunity and strength. To quote Robert Browning in "Rabbi ben Ezra"—

"Grow old along with me.
The best is yet to be,
The last of life,
For which the first was made."

[While all of us look at issues of employment for our ever-increasing population and we look at issues of improving the quality of life through better infrastructure, better medical facilities, better education, by and large, the issue of the quality of life in old age is not focused upon.]

[Today, in India 'inclusive growth' has become an immediate importance as the gap between the rich and poor widens. Moreover, the gap between the economically-active and the economically-inactive poor will also widen as the working population ages and is unable to provide for its subsistence. The Government's efforts have been, therefore, towards financial inclusion of the citizens, living in rural areas of India by making available to them the benefits of the financial branches, as in rural areas, which provide coverage to 40% of the population. The Government's endeavour is to ensure banking facilities to all habitations which have a population in excess of 2000 by March, 2012. The Swabhiman Programme launched by the Government is to bring about a closer relationship with financial sector to the people living in small rural village through banking correspondents.]

[More than 2 million people today, in Bangladesh receive old-age allowance. In Thailand, nearly 6 million people are covered by universal pension. China is rolling out a quasi-social pension to reach 100 million citizens. In Brazil and South Africa, social pensions are backed by constitution and form the basis of re-distributive policy.]

[The Government launched the New Pension System for its civil servants with effect from 1st January, 2004. It realized that not only the civil servants, but other citizens should also get that coverage of a national pension policy, which is driven on a non-profit basis by the Government. As a result, on 1st May, 2009, the NPS was extended to all citizens of India on a voluntary basis. Thereafter, looking at the need for covering economically backward or small investors, who had the means to support themselves during the economically-productive life but had no savings or pensions to fall back upon in case of ill health and old age, the Government introduced the NPS-Lite at a reduced cost with identical safety features for the small investors. The scheme was launched on 26th September, 2010.]

Ms. Rani Singh Nair belongs to the Indian Revenue Service. She has worked in the Ministry of Finance in the field of financial regulation. Her area of expertise is regulation, both in terms of Expenditure and Financial Management, as also formulation and implementation of Tax Policy.

Currently on deputation, she is Executive Director, Pension Fund Regulatory and Development Authority (PFRDA). She has been involved in the implementation of NPS not only in the Government sector but also conceptualization and implementation of NPS-Lite for the economically disadvantaged section of society. She has worked extensively for expansion of pension coverage to the unorganized worker.

(The views expressed in the article are the writer's own views)

15

Diabetes in the Elderly: A Growing Problem in India

Dr. V. Mohan

Introduction

Individuals, at extremes of life are always more vulnerable. Thus, the newborn and the elderly are particularly prone to illness: the former because body functions are not yet fully developed and the latter because they suffer from progressive decline of all body functions.

Diabetes mellitus, is fast reaching epidemic proportions in India and aging is one of significant factors driving this epidemic. The prevalence of diabetes mellitus begins to rise steadily from early adulthood, reaching a plateau in those aged 60 years or older. It is estimated that diabetes affects 10 - 25% of elderly people worldwide, with particularly high rates in populations such as Pima Indians, Mexican - Americans and South Asians (more specifically Indians). Regarding the scenario in India, studies in urban areas have shown that prevalence of diabetes in the elderly (>60 years) was nearly 30%. In addition, almost an equal proportion of elderly people have prediabetes (a forerunner to diabetes).

The frequency of hospitalization is also two to three times higher among elderly people with diabetes, compared to their counterparts without diabetes. Moreover, elderly persons with diabetes impose considerable economic, social and health burden on the community. This article will deal with some of the problems, peculiar to diabetes in the elderly.

Why does Diabetes Prevalence Increase with Age?

This is attributed to a combination of insulin resistance and decreased insulin secretion, both of which contribute to a steep increase in diabetes prevalence with age. However, may it give some consolation to the readers, that about 30-40% of the elderly population will never develop diabetes. This is because, a genetic background is usually needed to develop diabetes. In those who have this genetic defect, environmental factors like obesity, physical inactivity, unhealthy diet, stress and diabetogenic medications can trigger the onset of diabetes. Coexisting illnesses such as hypertension, coronary heart disease and stroke further increase the risk of functional disability and even premature death in elderly people with diabetes.

Presentation at the time of Diagnosis

The presence of diabetes in older people is varied but is often insidious, which may lead to a delay in diagnosis of the condition. It could vary from a totally asymptomatic presentation, to just tiredness to marked symptoms like thirst, weight loss, giddiness or confusion. Shoulder or joint pain, skin problems or occurance with other diseases e.g. tuberculosis, are not uncommon manifestations in the elderly. Many cases are detected just by finding a high blood sugar reading during routine investigations for other illnesses or during a master health check up.

Diagnosis

We recommended that all elderly individuals should be screened annually for diabetes. The diagnostic criteria for diabetes in the elderly, is essentially the same as for the young adults. An oral glucose tolerance test (GTT) is the ideal test, However, if this is not feasible, then a fasting plasma glucose can be done. A fasting plasma glucose value, greater than 126 mg/dl or a 2 hour value over 200 mg/dl in a GTT, is diagnostic of diabetes. For opportunistic screening, e.g., testing at places of worship, beaches, parks, offices, etc., even a random capillary blood glucose test using a glucometer would suffice. Anyone with a random blood glucose test of over 200 mg/dl on two occasions, has diabetes and treatment can be started. If the value is over 140 mg/dl, they can be advised to undergo further diagnostic testing like a GTT.

Acute Metabolic Complications

Older subjects with diabetes, are prone to a condition called hyperosmolar hyperglycemic state. Precipitating factors include infections, myocardial infarction, stroke and drugs such as thiazides or steroids. This condition is treatable, but concomitant illnesses such as pneumonia and heart attack, could make the prognosis grave.

Older patients are particularly susceptible to low blood glucose reactions (hypoglycaemia). Multiple factors underlie the increased susceptibility to hypoglycemia in the elderly, including kidney or liver impairment, inadequate food intake, erratic timings of meals or wrong doses of insulin taken inadvertently.

Chronic Diabetic Complications

Diabetic Eye Disease

Cataract, the most frequent cause of deteriorating vision

in the elderly, is more common in subjects with diabetes. Visual loss due to age-related macular degeneration, is also common in older patients with diabetes. However, diabetic retinopathy, or affection of the blood vessels in the back portion of the eye, is the commonest diabetes related eye problem. Hence, screening of the eyes (retinal check up) must be done on an annual basis in all people with diabetes. Those with long diabetes duration associated renal disease, high blood pressure or a history of foot infection, should be particularly screened for diabetic retinopathy. Diabetic retinopathy is an eminently treatable condition, if detected early.

Diabetic Foot Disease

Decreased blood circulation due to peripheral vascular disease, decreased sensation in the foot due to diabetic neuropathy, and high foot pressures due to foot deformities, are important factors contributing to the development of foot complications in elderly diabetic patients. Hence, a regular examination of the feet of all elderly diabetic patients, is of paramount importance.

Coronary Heart Disease and Cerebrovascular Disease

Heart attacks, heart failure and stroke are substantially more common in elderly subjects with diabetes compared to age-matched subjects without diabetes. Many elderly patients with diabetes may have a "silent heart attack" i.e., no chest pain at all. Such patients may present with breathlessness or tiredness, instead of the typical symptoms of chest pain.

Depression

Irrespective of age, gender or coexistent chronic disorders, depression is more often associated with diabetes.

Depression, not only significantly increases the risk of diabetes, but also worsens its control. Depression in diabetes can be treated successfully with pharmacotherapy, and/or psychologic counselling. Some drugs for depression are however known to increase body weight and worsen the diabetic status.

Management of Diabetes

Treatment Targets

Blood glucose goals for older adults may be relaxed as it is important to avoid low sugar readings. This is particularly true for patients with advanced diabetes complications, life-limiting co-morbid illness or substantial cognitive or functional impairment. These patients are less likely to benefit from tight diabetes control, but more likely to suffer serious adverse effects due to hypoglycaemia i.e. low blood glucose levels. Blood glucose goals should, therefore be individualized, keeping in mind the risk/ benefit ratios of the different treatment regimens. The glycated haemoglobin (HbA1c) test, is an excellent index of long term diabetes control. A value below 7% indicates good control of diabetes.

Although control, of hyperglycemia may be important in older individuals with diabetes, greater reductions in morbidity and mortality may result from control of other cardiovascular risk factors, than just tight glycemic control alone. Thus, in elderly patients, medicines like statins (to reduce blood cholesterol), and aspirin (to reduce risk of heart attack) along with blood pressure lowering drugs, should be judiciously used wherever indicated.

The American Geriatric Society has laid down guidelines for improving the care of the older person with diabetes. Patient education programmes can be really helpful for long term management of diabetes.

Treatment Options

Treatment options for diabetes include oral hypoglycemic agents and insulin. All anti-diabetic drugs should be used cautiously, as episodes of hypoglycemia may be severe and prolonged in the elderly because, counter - regulatory responses may be impaired in the elderly.

Sulfonylureas are often the first-line drugs used in people with diabetes because they are cheap and generally well tolerated. Their main hazard is hypoglycemia. Hence longer acting drugs like glibenclamide should be avoided in the elderly.

Metformin does not cause hypoglycemia or weight gain, and is inexpensive. However, it is contraindicated in renal impairment, hepatic or cardiac failure, and severe acute illness.

Other anti-diabetic drugs include acarbose, pioglitazone and newer drugs like sitagliptin or vildagliptin. The cost, side effects and safety of these drugs, must be kept in mind before prescribing them to the elderly.

Better standards of care in hospitals and in primary care, have made it easier and safer to use insulin in the treatment of older people with diabetes. The main indication for insulin is when the metabolic targets are not achieved with diet, exercise and oral agents. Insulin should also be used in acute situations such as heart attack, stroke and during major surgeries.

The main disadvantages of insulin is hypoglycaemia and weight gain, but benefits include improvements in well - being and quality of life. Rapid acting insulin analogs such as insulin lispro or insulin aspart, may cause less hypoglycemia and also have the advantage that they can be given after eating, especially where timing of meals are unpredictable. Some insulin pens have audible clicks for counting doses. Insulin should be started at the lowest dose and gradually titrated up until targets are reached.

Paramedic/Family Support

Effective delivery of diabetes care depends on a close cooperation between the family and the physician / diabetes specialists, with the help of nurses or other paramedical support staff. Elderly people with diabetes in care homes, are particularly vulnerable and require greater supervision and support in performing their daily activiities.

Medical Nutrition Therapy

Dietary compliance is often not feasible for the elderly because their disabilities may make it difficult for them even to prepare basic meals. Many elderly diabetic patients have insufficient caloric intake because of diminished appetite. Consultation with a dietician or home visits by social workers, can be helpful in the situation.

Conclusions

A diabetes service based on specialized teams comprising of physician / diabetologist, geriatrician, social worker, diabetes educator or dietician, can help to provide optimal care against diabetes, for the elderly. Rehabilitation programs are important for patients disabled by various complications such as amputation, peripheral neuropathy, immobility, stroke or cognitive changes. Health care for elderly must be cost - effective, which presents a difficult challenge for those with diabetes, because of its multiple co-morbidities. Emotional and psychological sequelae, add to the problem. However, with increased awareness and education regarding diabetes and with the support of family or friends, a useful and healthy life is possible for the elderly persons with diabetes.

16

Older Women: Do they Need Special Attention by Policy Makers

The UN Perspective

Ever since population aging became an issue to be concerned about, UN has been impressing upon member countries that though stemming from the same base, the issues faced by older men and older women are different, and have to be approached from different perspectives, instead of viewing aging as a common phenomenon among both sexes and attempting a common approach towards it. UN further held that, in formulating ageing policies, women's issues and concerns should receive priority. Thus, at the First World Assembly on Aging (1982) itself, UN declared. "The situation of older women everywhere must be a priority for policy action. Recognizing the differential impact of ageing on women and men is integral to ensuring full equality between women and men and to the development of effective and efficient measures to address the issue. It is therefore, crucial to ensure the integration of a gender perspective into all policies, programmes and legislation." Again in the 94th Plenary Meeting of The United Nations (23 December 1994) UN exhorted member countries–"to ensure that older women's concerns and contributions to development are recognized and incorporated into the strategies, programmes and policies of the Platform for Action which deals with quality, development and peace. These concerns and contributions should be considered under three main agenda items of the Summit: Elimination of Poverty, Social Integration and Employment". This appeal for gender perspective on ageing problems was continued by UN in all the later meetings.

The Convention for Eradication of Discrimination Against Women (CEDAW) in 2002, endorsed this recommendation of the UN, and further declared that "Both men and women face discrimination due to old age but women experience ageing differently. Gender relations structure the entire life cycle from birth to old age, influencing access to resources and opportunities and shaping life choices at every stage. Good health, economic security and adequate housing are essential requirements of ageing with dignity. But, older women in both developed and developing countries face difficulties in accessing these, on the basis of equality with men. "Older women's" needs vary according to their age and physical condition. Policy makers need to recognize this reality and take it into account. Women tend to suffer disproportionately from various forms of discrimination and, ageing makes this situation more complex. CEDAW further points out that special programmes should be tailored to address the physical, mental, emotional and health needs of older women in rural areas, with special focus on women belonging to minorities and women with disabilities. CEDAW also points out that access to free health care services is very important for older women in order to enjoy a satisfactory standard of mental and physical health. Older women face a high risk of chronic illness and disability as well as, from degenerative diseases such as osteoporosis and cervical cancer.

Finally, CEDAW warns that Older women must not be viewed as victims, but recognized for the positive economic and social contributions they have made throughout their lives, both to their families and to society at large. They must also be valued independently for their economic contributions. They must not be subjected to discrimination on the ground of gender. Also, they should not be viewed only as beneficiaries, but also as contributors to development.

The Indian View

The GOI, even though a member of the CEDAW Convention as well as of the 'UN Declarations on Aging', has not been able to do much to conform to the UN or CEDAW resolutions. This is clear from India's Country Report on CEDAW (2002), and also the 2nd NGO Shadow Report on CEDAW (2006).

To be sure, India has certainly forged ahead in the matter of empowerment of women. The National Women's Commission, the National Rural Employment Guarantee Act (NREGA) and various women empowerment programmes such as DWACRA, IRDP, JRY and the latest in the series, the Self Help Groups (SHGs) are examples. The 11th Five Year Plan Draft Approach Paper (June 2006) mentioned about the need for gender balancing, and called for special focus on three aspects - violence against women, economic empowerment and women's health. The National Rural Health Mission (NRHM) is also heavily women oriented. While, it may be argued that these cover older women also, old women have not been in focus in these programmes and, there does not seem to be an appreciation that older women's issues are different and require special focus instead of viewing them as part of women's problems in general. The manner in which older women are treated in the National

Policy on Older Person, also reflects the conventional attitude. In a passing manner (Section 11) it mentions the problem of lack of care givers, due to industrialization and urbanization and, also education and employment of women outside the home. "The position of single persons, particularly females, is more vulnerable in old age, as few persons are willing to take care of non, linear relatives". It also complains about "widows, an overwhelming majority of whom have no independent source of income, do not own assets and are totally dependent". But the policy document does not speak of the deeper concerns of older women in the social, economic and health fields and is equally silent on them, on the action side (except a passing reference in Para 65 on widows' right to inheritance, occupancy and disposal of property). The policy makers cannot be blamed for this, as the demographers and social scientists and even activists, did not see any uniqueness in older women's issues. In fact, policy makers and *social researchers have continued* to treat the older population as a homogeneous group and to assume that what is good for older men is equally good for older women and no special attention needs to be vested on older women's problems and needs. This attitude, of course, is not confined to India, but is a worldwide phenomenon, especially in the developing countries. This is evident from the several exhortations of the United Nations and its bodies, as shown in the passages quoted above.

The fact is that there are several areas where the position of older women differs, basically from that of men. I shall take four major fields, namely, demographic, social, economic, and health to demonstrate this argument.

The Demographic Scene

The outstanding demographic factor in sex distribution

is the out numbering of women over men in the older population. UN figures estimate that the number of older people in 2050 will be over 2 billion, which will be 22% of the global population at that time. The majority of older persons are women, their percentage being - 55. 80% men (over 60) are married against 48% older women. There are 82 men for every 100 women at the age of 60, but only 55 men for every 100 women at the age of 80. This phenomenon of older women out numbering older men, is due to differential longevity of life for men and women. In more developed countries like Japan, the expectation of life at birth for a man is 74, and for a woman 78. Living longer may look like a boon, but not for old women, especially in the developing countries for at least four reasons. Much of their life is spent in morbidity, poverty and widowhood and worse still, without proper food, shelter, and health care. There is nearly total absence of old age social security for women in these countries.

The Social Dimension

Perhaps, it is in the social sphere that an old woman suffers most. Unlike an old man, who can at least carry the notion of male superiority till he is completely disabled, for whatever reason, a woman begins to lose her image and position in the household, once she is branded as old or appears to be so. Older women suffer from the quadruple disadvantages - being old, being poor, being widowed, and being stricken with frailty due to prolongation of life. The social construction of old age, makes a woman different from man. Though, chronologically both woman and man are treated as old from the age of 60 onwards, physically they enter old age with two different outfits. By the time a woman reaches the age of 60, the problems of aging would have already made their ravages on her, more heavily than on her male counterpart. Her movements are restricted to the four walls of the household and, this cuts all social ties with the outside world, which she had enjoyed so far. This applies to all situations of going out - to social gatherings, get-togethers, places of worship - in fact, to all events outside the household. Even within the family, visitors are discouraged from seeing her, especially if she is frail or not in a presentable situation. Ageing has different meanings for men and women. This is as much socially defined as in actual life practice.

Widowhood is another handicap of women. In a patriarchal society, widows and widowers live in two different worlds - the former in a world of privations and, the latter in a world of priviledges. There are more widows among older women, than there are widowers among older men and as age increases, this proportion increases rapidly. Around 63% women are widowed at the age of 60, in contrast to, 22% men in that age. At 80, more than 84% women are widows against 32% men. Unlike a widower who can get a second wife more easily, a widow cannot get a match easily, as widow remarriage is socially discouraged if not forbidden. Hence, even a very young widow will have to remain in that condition for life.

Widows suffer from manifold handicaps even in the prime of their life, and when they get old, they are treated more unkindly. Even today, in some countries in Africa, for example, in Malawi and Tanzania, many older widows in rural areas are subjected to allegations of witchcraft and face the risk of death from lynching. In Botswana, older widows have to wear ugly clothing to mourn their husbands' death. Conditions in India were only slightly better in the past, even though of late, these have improved a lot. Even so, the old prejudices of society against widows, still continue. The condition of widows in Kerala, which has a long history of women's education and social status, is not as rosy as one would expect, would illustrate this.

In the matter of elderly abuse in India, studies have shown that abuse is more on older women than on older men. All sorts of abuses ranging from taunts and more aggressive forms of psychological (mental) abuse, physical abuse including beating and infliction of grievous injuries, denial of food, shelter and health care and, worse still, total neglect and abandonment are reported from all over India, especially, from urban areas. Abuse cuts across education and economic status of both the victim and the abuser, and also kinship ties. Most abuses take place within the four walls of the family and are perpetrated by the son or son-in-law (and occasionally by grand children) and, they mainly centre around transfer of property or assets. Since, the aggressor does not expect retaliation from the old and fragile lady, the abuse would continue either till the perpetrator achieves the end or till the victim breathes her last.

Existing laws, including the more recent-Maintenance and Welfare of Parents and Senior Citizens Act 2007, have not been found to be advantageous to women as to men, again because of the prejudice of the administrative machinery and of the wider society, towards women and also because, of the many inhibitions and proscriptions that women have, in taking up issues with the courts and the Police. For these reasons, women do not come forward with complaints as much as men. Being invisible, their problems are little known outside the family and even when known, people are not as enthusiastic in their case as in the case of men. Hence, civil society organizations do not intervene in their case, even though there is provision for third party intervention in the

Maintenance of Parents Act. Our enquiries regarding this Act, showed that women do not complain about the misdeeds of their sons/daughters or in-laws because a woman does not want her kin to be hauled before the Police or Court of Law, however much she is subjected to deprivations and cruelties by them, while men do not show such qualms towards misbehaving sons/daughters. We found from several quarters that the motherly instinct takes primacy in women over insults and injuries."I do not want to register any formal complaint with the Tribunal (under the Act, 2007) even though I am suffering from the worst form of neglect coupled with insults and threats, because this will affect the future of my dear child whom I nourished and brought up as the pupil of my eye. I will suffer this as my fate; how many more years do I have in this world?". Take the situation of men. To begin with, abuse by kin against them is fewer than towards women because of their very gender; they would fight back; men are more mobile and, have circles outside the family where they could bring their complaints. They are more visible and can also make their problems visible, which would by itself act as a deterrent against abuse.

Economic Situation

Poverty is the twin sister of a woman. The adage "feminization of poverty" proclaims this loudly. In the case of old women, this works with added disadvantage: (1) her capacity for work would have diminished with age and, no one would like to hire an unproductive or near-unproductive women; (2) she would not have made any savings for the rainy day because like most other women, she had been working in the unorganized sector with no social security of any sort for old age; and (3) the laws of inheritance are heavily loaded against her. In many cases, her share of ancestral property is lesser than that for male members. She cannot inherit the property of her late husband. Even if she has property or other assets, she requires male assistance to manage it. This is true not only of land or building but also of other forms of savings, for example a bank account, because her immobility (or limited mobility) on the one hand and, possible frailty on the other, would not permit her to move outside home and operate a bank account independently, by herself. In the case of rural and poor women, such modern facilities are irrelevant.

There are several empowerment programmes for women in India - the JRY, DWCRA, IRDP, NREGA and the latest SHG. But, none of these women focused programmes takes the older woman into account. Naturally, none of the woman empowerment programmes, has done justice to old women.

National Sample Surveys have found that more old women are dependent on their children than old men, and this, coupled with the fact that a third of the Indian families is living below poverty line, makes the lot of the dependent old woman more pathetic. In some States in India, only one member of a destitute family is eligible for old age pension and this, most of the time, works against women who are sidelined in awarding pension. The marginalized nature of women is indicated by the data from old age homes. The majority of the inmates of old age homes in India are women, which is indicative of many things. More of them are destitute compared to men, and families find themselves unable to look after them, and hence, are compelled to leave them in an old age home. Besides destitution, the other major reasons are neglect or abandonment by family members, even when well-to-do because, they are found to be a burden to the younger generation. In some cases, the old woman herself volunteers to go to an old age home because she finds herself increasingly distanced in the family. All these result in the presence of a larger number of older women than men, in the old age homes.

Health Scenario

In the sphere of health also, older women stand in a uniquely disadvantageous position compared to older men. There are several sides to this disadvantage.

To begin with, older women suffer from most, if not all of the ailments that old men suffer. But, older women carry more chronic diseases while older men carry more acute diseases. Chronic diseases, are difficult to cure and treatment is expensive and prolonged. Post-menopausal conditions and ailments, are another set of diseases peculiar to women. Women live longer than men and so, they have an extended period of morbidity and poor health (expansion of morbidity syndrome). Though, men and women die fundamentally from more or less identical generic causes, the rates differ, i.e., the pace of death differs much more than the cause of death. Even when both sexes have identical patterns of morbidity, they suffer differently. Women have higher incidence rate for most non-fatal diseases whereas, men have higher incidence rate for fatal diseases. There are also other dimensions of morbidity where men and women differ widely. As mentioned earlier, the major one is in the matter of reproductive health. The gender specific illness, of earlier ages, accumulate and make joint and aggressive assault on women in old age. Post-menopausal syndromes including osteoporosis and osteo/rheumatic arthritis, emerge as prominent illness among them during this period. The situation is compounded by the fact that most women take their diseases for granted, and, suffer them stoically. Women try to live with their ailments to the maximum extent possible, and, complain about them only when the illness is no longer bearable. Also, most women think that these ailments are part of their gender-related problems, accelerated by old age and that, as women they have to live with them. On the other hand, men are prone to exaggerate even small ailments and, demand immediate medical attention. Further, they get preference over women in attention and treatment. Also, old women do not get proper care givers when ill, as they have been care givers for others. The erosion of the joint family system and the emergence of the nuclear family, leave no care giver in the family to look after an old woman. This happens when they need a bystander, whether in home or in hospital. One of the major factors for women's increased morbidity is their longer life span. Even though this phenomenon is only slowly catching up in India due to the county's slower pace of development, it is bound to appear in the country over the years, as the situation in Kerala has shown. In Kerala, the life span of women is three-to-four years more than that of men. As women are more frail than men, the increased years of life are fraught with more diseases. This is also revealed in the Kerala case.

A little recognized fact about woman's illness is the occupational diseases which are peculiar to women and, which afflict them in old age. The majority of agricultural workers in India are women and, most of them work in the open fields. Women's work in the agricultural sector creates specific health problem; they spend long hours standing in water during weeding and transplanting, thus becoming vulnerable in that process to infectious and parasitic diseases, arthritis and rheumatism. An equally more dangerous hazard is that contributed by chemical fertilizers, which spill into the water in which they work and poisonous pesticides which fill the air they breath for long hours. Work during harvesting time involves long time stooping and, such conditions accentuate back pain and osteo-arthritic complaints.

In the normal course, the differential pattern of disease prevalence in men and women should be a lesson to health management experts for gender-focused geriatric care, but in India, the gender factor is underplayed or assumed away. There is hardly any focus on health of older women in India's health policy or health care system, including the lately introduced National Rural Health Mission (NRHM) and the National Programme for the Health Care of the Elderly (NPHCE).

Gender makes discrimination in the medical management of women. Other things being equal, priority for health care and for costly treatment is given to men over women. The other side of the picture is that an ailing woman (with or without other handicaps), is more unwelcome to the family than an ailing man.

Thus, on all counts, older women are at a great disadvantage compared to older men and unless this fact is accepted and provided for in policies and programmes, their conditions will only worsen. Since, their number is going to be progressively on the rise in the years ahead along with the accentuation of the problems described, this will have wider consequences in terms of human rights and social justice.

How to Empower Older Women?

A national consultation on empowerment of older women in India organized by the Centre for Gerontological

Studies in Thiruvnanthapuram in March 2011, has brought to light several suggestions for the empowerment of women in India, especially in the sphere of social care and health care. The most prominent among them are given below along with others, as they have come out of the combined wisdom of experts from the different disciplines.

An old woman is more organically bound to the family than an old man, and, this has to be taken into account in any programme for the empowerment of older women. This has much to do with "ageing in place" which has been a key UN formula in the well-being of older persons. The first thing that should be done in this regard, is to make the old woman acceptable in the family. The old woman becomes unwelcome in the family mainly for two reasons. One, of course, is her inability to contribute to the family pool and, the other is her health condition.

One reason for the unwelcomeness or non-acceptance of an old woman in the family, is the economic burden that an unproductive and expensive (expensive because of the cost of her Medicare) old woman brings to the family. The burden is heaviest in the case of poor and destitute families. The currently given old age pension is very small and is confined to BPL families, though it is a source of consolation for the old, regarding their self-worth and contribution.

To circumvent this, all old women irrespective of their economic status should be given a minimum pension and, the amount should be 20% more than that for men and staggered according to age. i.e., 20% increase after 70 years, 50% increase after 80 years and, double after 100 years. The increase is warranted by the increased expenses for the old woman, on account of extra-physical and medical needs, as age increases. The minimum pension, thus given should be adequate for meeting the reasonable expenses of the old woman, including health care expenses.

A family that has to hire the services of a home nurse for the old kin, either for reasons of proven disability or dementia, should be given a supplementary allowance.

All BPL old women and all old widows and, those old staying alone or with spouse-only irrespective of their income status, should be given free ration from the PDS.

A BPL family maintaining an old (or olds), should be given appropriate quantity of free ration from the public distribution system (PDS). Similarly placed APL families should be given ration at heavily subsidized rates.

All old women from BPL families, should be given one full and balanced meal a day, through the ICDS system or a system created for this purpose. This is not only to alleviate their hunger, but also to assure minimum nutrition for them. Most old women are found to suffer from nutritional anemia which is also a major cause of death for them.

All 80 'plus' women, irrespective of their income status, should be exempted from payment of income tax, should be given free journey passes in the Railways and public transport system. Where warranted, an attendant on such women should also be given free pass, when visiting hospitals and other service providing agencies.

A scheme similar (or parallel) to the prevailing Women's Self Help Groups (SHG) scheme, may be started for those women who need/are willing to work. This will achieve three purposes: (1) a feeling of self - worth and productive ageing; (2) power and dignity; and (3) freedom from monotony of being secluded at home. Government should not only sponsor and supervise the system, but should also provide necessary financial support and/or, bank guarantee towards capital. Micro finance facilities should be extended to them. Financial institutions are unwilling to give credit to older persons and especially, older women, and hence the need for government guarantee.

A website may be created from where details of jobs available to older women, could be collected and made available to the old women who have access to internet facility. Such jobs that could be done at home or that areconvenient to them could be taken up by those whoso desire. This will help to help some of the APL women to be employed in meaningful and productive jobs.

For those who are confined to their homes either due to immobility, morbidity or other reasons and are, in bad shape, there should be some monitoring mechanism to ensure their wellbeing. A Neighbourhouod Club of old persons will be an appropriate agency to do this. Members of the Club could visit them, ensure their welfare and help mitigate their sufferings. If the woman is abused or neglected, these members could use their influence on the kin, to behave properly. Their visits will be a threat and warning to the delinquent kin, to correct themselves. These visits will also provide a social bond and give a feeling of companionship with age-mates to the immobile women, who would be otherwise isolated.

In many cities in India, destitute women and those with mental problem, are left to wander on the streets, begging for food and, being in a state of utter neglect and abandonment. These women should be identified and placed in shelter homes or old age homes. The role of old age homes is quite relevant to them, as they cannot get care from any other place. Some of them may not be acceptable in an old age home because of some mental problem, they should be accommodated in a neighbourhood geriatric home.

One of the major reasons that makes the presence of the old woman in the family unwelcome is her health condition. If the woman is immobilized for life and, requires a bystander all the time and huge expenditure on medicine, the family in most cases would not be comfortable with her. This has to be noted against the fact that an old woman suffers double marginalization if poor and sickly. Hence, great attention has to be paid, to the health of the old woman, to make her acceptable to the family.

One way to achieve this is to provide universal health insurance to all old, with focus on the health care of women. Health insurance should be flexible - free for the BPL and heavily subsidized for others. Insurance coverage should be 50% more for women than men, whether BPL or APL.

A programme similar to that recently introduced in Kerala (the programme of Vayomithram), by which mobile medical units travel in the different parts of the city and, give care to homebound elderly, will go a long way in mitigating the problem of immobile and sick elderly, especially in poor families.

In hospitals with geriatric wards, a certain number of beds should be earmarked for old women. Further, both NRHM and NPHCE should be made older-women friendly.

The legal system of the country is not very women-friendly, notwithstanding the fact that there are several laws protecting the rights of the elderly. To begin with and as the CEDAW Convention points out, "In reality older women are invisible in the application of human rights law". Most old women are ignorant of the laws protecting their rights, and, even those who know them, seldom go to the court of law to get relief. The reasons are many. Patriarchal bias of those handling the law, old woman's hesitation to haul an erring son or daughter to the court or policestation at the fag end of her life with no certainty about the outcome, and, the long drawn procedure involved in litigation - these and many others are minus factors in women going for legal remedies. In this context, the enactment of the Maintenance and Welfare of Parents and Senior Citizens Act 2007, should be considered a boon. But, here also there are some weak spots. The new legislation has not been adopted by all States and Union Territories in India. Some States have notified but, not enacted it; some others which have enacted the law, have not appointed the requisite personnel for its enforcement. It is necessary that all States enact the law and enforce it vigorously in spirit and letter. Though the act is gender-neutral, it is necessary that special concern is shown on issues relating to old women, especially in bringing them to the eye of justice, as more women than men are the victims of abuse and neglect. It is necessary that those concerned with the enforcement of the Act, should be sensitized in older women's issues and concerns.

A woman should have the right to 50% of the family income/property, earned by the husband and wife together after marriage, and on separation/divorce or death of husband, should be additionally eligible for 50% of the personal wealth of the husband, irrespective of any will that he would have made to the contrary. A uniform civil code should be made for the entire country for this purpose, guaranteeing, among other things, equal share in the family property to all members.

Removing Ageism - The Stereotyping of Aging

Ageism or stereotyping of ageing, has played more havoc on older women than an older men. The caricature of an old woman is that of a hag without any positive virtues but with all vices, especially if she happens to be a widow, which is the case with most women in advanced ages. Hence, this negative stereotyping of the old and, especially old women, has to be done away with from the social mindset. This cannot be achieved over a short time. For this, the potential of a lot of agencies, especially the media and the school system, has to be brought in. Promoting positive and favourable attitudes and mindsets among all sections of the society, including older persons, is vital to removing the thinking and behavior based on ageism.

17

Micro Finance Services for Older Persons: Needs, Policy Issues and Strategies

Dr. Navin Anand

In December 1990, the United Nations General Assembly designated 1st October as the International Day of Older Persons. Subsequently, the General Assembly of United Nations through its resolution 46/91 dated 16 December, 1991 declared some principles for older persons and encouraged governments to incorporate the principles into their national programmes. There are two principles that are directly related to livelihoods of older persons :

- Older persons should have the opportunity to work or to have access to other income generating opportunities; and
- Older persons should be able to participate in determining when and at what pace withdrawal from the labour force takes place.

For UN, older persons' welfare has always been a concern. In 2002, the Second World Assembly on Ageing adopted the Madrid International Plan of Action on Ageing, to respond to the opportunities and challenges of population ageing in the 21st century, and, to promote the development of a society for all ages. Further, the theme of the year 2010's commemoration "Older persons and the achievement of the Millennium Development Goals (MDGs)" also reveals the focus of the UN on older persons and its importance in MDGs.

A report of Department of Economic and Social Affairs of the United Nations Secretariat reveals an important fact that the number of people aged 60 and over worldwide, is expected to triple to 1.9 billion[1] by 2050. More importantly, most of the increase in the older population is taking place in low-income countries, where the average income is less than US$2 per day. Population projection for 1996-2016 made by technical group on population projections (1996) indicate that the 100 million mark is expected to be reached in 2013. Projection beyond 2016 made by United Nations (1996 revision) has indicated that India will have 198 million person, 60+ in 2030 and, 326 million in 2050.[2] This statistics shows that in developing countries, more focused efforts are required to address the issues related to older persons.

Defining 'Older Persons'

As per United Nations, an older person is defined as someone over 60 years of age. The "oldest old" refers to those over 80, who comprise the fastest-growing old age group. At the global level, the average annual growth rate of persons aged 80 years or above (3.8 per cent), is currently twice as high as the growth rate of the population over 60 years of age (1.9 per cent). Currently, six countries account for 54 per cent of the total number aged 80 years or obove. They are China, with the largest number (12 million), United States of America (9 million), India (6 million), Japan (5 million), Germany (3 million) and Russian Federation (3 million).[3] The rapid growth of the 'oldest old' among the older population in India makes it more important to have an appropriate policy for these people.

In developing countries, the labour force participation among the older population is considerably higher than in developed countries. This is mainly, because of the lack of adequate pension and retirement programmes in most developing countries. As per a report of International Labour Organization (ILO, 2000), in many developing countries there are still large concentrations of older workers in agriculture and in the informal sector, both of which are generally not covered by social security systems or pensions. There are studies[4] that show that older people are amongst the most socially excluded and chronically poor.

Key Issues Related to Micro Finance and Livelihoods

Microfinance services for the older men and women, living in rural and urban areas, are as important as serving any other segment of the society. The microfinance needs of older persons include savings and deposit services; credit for emergencies, consumption and income generation activities; Leasing services; Insurance (Life, health and general insurance); Micro Pensions; and remittances/ payment services. Older people have limited access to microfinance institutions (MFIs) and banks, and therefore to microfinance services. There are various bottlenecks and problems faced by older people in getting MF and livelihood support services —

1. Older Persons - Not Considered as Valid Customers

In the present scenario, older persons are not been considered valid customers of microfinance. Many MFIs have a policy of denying loans to customers who are around 60 years or above. This has increased after the introduction of credit insurance. Many a times, even long standing customers are refused loans, as they reach 60 years of age.

A report of Help Age India also confirms the fact that older people are not considered credit-worthy, and are therefore, denied access to cost-effective formal institutional credit.[5] This requires initiatives from government and regulatory bodies, in the form of having clear policies and regulations for the MFIs, on providing services to the older persons and not restricting older people to get MF services.

MFIs can focus on strengthening their portfolio quality to cater to the needs of the older people. It is true that if the loans are not insured, bankers show reluctance to give loans to MFIs. In case of older persons, insurance coverage should not be a compulsory condition in getting a loan. MFIs/banks can review the track record of old customers and offer loans without insurance cover. The proposed Microfinance (Development and Regulation) Bill, 2011 does not specifically mention anything about catering MF services to the older people.

2. Face problems due to low proximity to banks in Remote areas

In various discussions and reports, examples of the low proximity to financial institutions and banks in the mountain and remote areas have been citied. In an e-discussion on Microfinance Community of Practice, United Nations, it was informed that in some cases pension holders travel even 100 kilometers to get their pension in North Eastern region, due to lack of banking facilities.

3. Do not have special coverage under finance schemes of Ministries

It has been observed that often in finance schemes of ministries and their various special projects, there is no special coverage for the older people. As a first step, it is important to consider that a large number of older people are socially excluded and vulnerable, and therefore, need to be covered in different schemes of financing. One positive trend that has been seen in last few years, is that in response to RBI's Senior Citizens Savings Scheme, 2004,[6] a number of nationalized and private banks have opted to provide special interest rates to the senior citizens on their fixed deposits.

4. Older persons often not included as member in SHGs

Microfinance services are largely covered under SHG bank linkage programme of NABARD, wherein, through commercial banks, Regional Rural banks and Cooperatives Banks, SHGs and JLGs are being supported, under the programme to provide microfinance to their members. It has largely been observed that older persons are often not included in the groups, and therefore, do not get MF services.

5. Problem in remittance and payments services

The pensioners, who are physically incapable, require savings services and pension distribution facility at the door steps. The efficacy and relevance of micro financial services for OPs will be limited, unless MF products and services like savings, deposit and remittance services are provided at the door steps. Many a times, OPs due to ill health or incapacity find it difficult to go to banks, so MF services could be provided at their door steps and can be made mandatory in such cases. Similarly, older persons face problems in making payments for the electric bills, water tax, house tax to government and other service providers. Systems of online payments have been introduced in some of the urban areas, however, in rural areas this is still a problem.

The delivery of microfinance services can be done through commercial banks, regional rural banks, cooperative banks, MFIs/MFOs, post offices and the new breed of

Business Correspondents/Facilitators linked to banks. Cooperatives have relative advantage of having a good network and functioning at the door steps of the rural masses. Post Offices also have similar setup and, can serve as Business Correspondents of banks. Moreover, MFIs, NGOs and Charitable Institutions having objective of working for OPs are also good source for providing multi-faceted services.

In order to fast track the process of making changes in the lives of the people, especially in context of having enhanced inclusion and effective microfinance services, a clear strategy of providing MF services to the poor is important.

Strategies for Covering Older People under MF Services

Segmenting Older Persons into different categories: Since, the socio-economic background of different subsets of older persons (OPs) and their needs are different, therefore, before planning and strategizing for their livelihood promotion and microfinance services, it is important to segment them using different criteria of classification—

- **Geographic location:** OPs living in Rural/ Urban / Mountain and Remote areas (The requirements and problems of the older persons living in rural areas are very different from that of urban. For example poor proximity to banks, low livelihood options are more relevant in rural areas compared to urban)
- **Gender** (Women OPs are more vulnerable than men)
- **Economic independence/ dependence** (Pension Holders; Non-Pension Holder but having support from Family; and Older people having low or no income)
- **Vulnerability** (Physically or mentally challenged and poor)

- **Marital status** (Married/ single men/women, widows)

The classification of older persons on various parameters will help in identifying needs, and, developing microfinance and livelihood related products and services. It is important, to address the issues of older women separately, as they seldom hold ownership of land and other properties which makes them more vulnerable.

Formation of ESHGs : There are special initiatives in many states like Bihar, Tamil Nadu, Himachal Pradesh (SAGP Project) and few other states, to form SHG of Elders called 'ESHGs'. Help Age India have also taken good initiatives in forming ESHGs in different states under its rural age care programme. A micro-finance institution of the elderly (SRmFIE) is also been promoted to provide MF services to OPs through ESHGs. Destitute elders are covered under a separate programme-'Sponsor-a-Gran programme' which also promotes groups for livelihood promotion.[7] Based on the experience of ESHGs in different states, it will be important to incorporate creation of ESHGs under National Rural Livelihood Mission, so as to cover older people under the programme.

Older People's Associations

It is clearly evident that for microfinance and other support services, formations of community based groups have been successfully experimented. Besides ESHGs, another form of community based institutions for the older people are – Older People's Associations (OPAs). These institutions are community based organizations formed to improve living conditions, social security and, delivering need based services to the older persons.

A comprehensive study of five countries including India on OPs reveals that *"In India, OPAs in both Bihar and Tamil*

Nadu were initially created as mechanisms for emergency response. In both locations, the OPAs have since, evolved into Elder Self-Help Groups (ESHGs) and focus on enabling older people to access regular savings accounts and low interest loans. For all older people, the low interest rate was seen as a positive reason to take a loan. Because Help Age India-supported ESHGs focus specifically on livelihood activities, the direct links between membership and improved livelihoods security were overt. An additional positive impact that ESHG members noted was improved self-esteem and respect from others in the community."[8]

Quick Survey of the socio-economic conditions of different segments: There is a need of a quick sample survey of the socio-economic conditions of senior citizens, to understand the practical and realistic conditions as well as different types of needs of OPs. This will be useful in deciding the products and services required by OPs, evolving a rehabilitation package and also, in prioritizing initiatives to be taken up by Government and other relevant agencies.

Mobile Branches — RBI's recent decision: RBI has recently taken a decision of allowing commercial banks to start mobile branches/ banking services in the remote areas, wherein, no approval of RBI is required, on case to case basis. The Mobile banks can be started in areas having less than 50,000 population and, not served by co-operative banks or regular branch of commercial banks. Through mobile phone banking, Biometric Smart Cards, Rural ATM services, MF services can be provided at door steps of older persons through technology innovations.

Banking Correspondents/ Banking Facilitators (BC/BF): RBI has introduced Banking Correspondent Model, so as to fast track financial inclusion. Successful implementation of this model can help older persons in getting

MF services at the door steps. Besides getting MF services, there will be a high potential of getting livelihoods as BC/BFs.

The BC/BF model needs changes in terms of providing sufficient margins to BCs/BFs. A number of forums have identified this issue, so that the model can be successfully taken up and more people join as BC/BFs.

A good model to refer in this context is 'Info Lady' model implemented under D.Net project (Development Research Network), Bangladesh. Through 'Info Lady' that functions as mobile information and service centre to provide livelihood related information to the rural poor families, multifaceted services are provided at the doorsteps. Even health check ups are being taken up by 'info lady' in rural areas. Similar experiment can be done for providing Microfinance and livelihood related services to the older people, especially older women.

Using Reverse Mortgage Schemes: Reverse Mortgage as a product, is fairly new to India. Dewan Housing Finance was among the forerunners to start reverse mortgage financing by introducing a product- 'Saksham'. Since then, most lending institutions/banks have come up with their own reverse mortgage products. Reverse mortgage schemes are useful for those older persons who are having properties in their names, but not having liquid money required at the time of emergencies, medical treatment, hospitalization or for regular consumption needs.

Conceptually, Reverse Mortgage seeks to monetize the house as an asset and specifically, the owner's equity in the house. The scheme involves the Senior Citizen borrower(s) mortgaging the house property to a lender, who then makes periodic payments to the borrower(s) during the latter's lifetime. Reverse Mortgage Loans (RMLs) are to be extended by Primary Lending Institutions (PLIs) viz. Scheduled Banks and Housing Finance Companies (HFCs) registered with NHB or, any other class of institutions, as may be notified by Government of India.[9]

The prescribed tenure for reverse financing is 15 years, and, the owner of the house and his/her spouse continues to live in the house till their death, which can occur later than the tenure of the reverse mortgage. Simply put, any senior citizen, opting for reverse mortgage will get annuity (the reverse EMI) from the bank for 15 years. This amount supplements the pension income, and help OPs to lead a comfortable life without depending on anyone.

The amount received through reverse mortgage is considered as loan and not income; hence, the same will not attract any tax liability. With duly drafted tripartite agreement between the concerned Bank, Borrower and MFI, the latter can create additional charge on the mortgaged property and, extend micro-credit to the person, as and when such requirement for small loan arises. Recent reports indicate that a very small percentage of senior citizens seem to have taken advantage of the facility, since its inception. This could be perhaps, because better awareness had not been created about the product. Secondly, the Indian banking industry caps the available loan amount at Rs. 50 lakh (Rs. 5 million), instead of providing for an equitable percentage of the property's value, and limits the loan period to a tenure of 15 years. The product is still evolving and may take on new dimensions, depending on how the banks wish to present its consumer appeal.

Older Persons' Cooperatives: One good option of providing microfinance services to the older persons could be to form multi-purpose cooperatives of older persons. These can be formed out of the ESHGs formed for OPs. The cooperatives of older people can be registered under Self

Reliant Cooperative Acts wherein, undertaking various MF activities is not restricted. These cooperatives can take up savings services also. Under proposed Microfinance (Development and Regulation) Bill 2011, these cooperatives are kept out of the purview of the RBI's regulations, meant for MFIs.

Special Government programmes: The social and financial security schemes and provisions such as widow pension, old age pension, housing etc. are seldom monitored or facilitated by the existing NGOs and micro credit groups. MFIs can play a role in becoming effective conduits, for delivery of these services and rights to the elders in their respective regions of operations. Special programmes may be designed in cooperation with some of the state Governments that have already taken good steps to fulfill social, economic, and health related needs of different OPs, especially single, divorced, widowed, unemployed older men and women.

Micro Finance for Livelihoods Promotion of Older Persons

Older persons are having a variety of skills and knowledge in the area of medicinal herbs, handicrafts and handlooms, pickle, papad and home made food production etc., but many of them are leading an idle life due to not having any capital. So, if government can provide support in the form of venture capital, then livelihoods for older persons can be promoted. MFIs can also think of creating a group of elders with varied expertise, and, fund them to undertake consultancy or undertake assignments to get some earnings.

Insurance Issues : Micro Health Insurance cover is denied by most of the Insurers for certain age group of people, especially older persons. Insurers consider OPs as 'most vulnerable claim prone group'. They also consider that insuring OPs will increase the claim ratio, and thereby, affect the profitability of their business. IRDA may consider including social security for OPs in its mandate. There is a need for evolving a specific Micro Health Insurance scheme for OPs after due analysis of the ongoing Micro Health Insurance (MHI) schemes.

Since, insurance cover is denied by many insurance companies after a certain age, 'Health Mutuals' has come out as a good substitute to provide health risk cover, including health care services. There have been few good experiments in India on Health mutuals, such as community owned Health Micro Insurance Model - Uplift Mutuals[10] that works successfully in Maharashtra.

Health Mutual Model has following positive features:

- Community owned groups, better able to meet the health needs of a specific community
- Healthcare services are provided at the right time, right cost and without risk of debt
- Limited possibility for health service providers to charge high prices for care
- Built-in monitoring system - 'Arogya Nidhi' is collectively operated by community representatives and NGOs/ promoting organization
- Focus is not on profit generation, distribution of profit or creating a shared capital base, but to cover poor from health related risks.

Applying 'Support Group' concept: One possibility that can be explored, in case of supporting older persons is-creation of support groups of well offs. These groups will be more feasible in urban and semi-urban areas. Members of the support group, will be in a position to help older persons and their groups in many ways, such as providing matching grant to ESHGs, technical support in the livelihood promotion, supporting groups in forging links with banks.

Conclusion

While segmentation of older persons in different categories will provide clarity about the specific needs of the older persons and, help in sketching demand based policies and programmes, innovations in microfinance initiatives will help in providing services to the older people at the door steps. MFIs can cover those OPs who are eligible, but not covered under Government schemes. There is a need of giving special privileges in respect to remittances, pensions and insurance services to widows and destitute. Development of a holistic 'social security system', and, plan for providing microfinance and livelihood services to the older persons is the need of the hour.

(**Note:** The paper is based on the results of the E-discussion on National Policy on Older Persons, in Microfinance Community of Practice, Solution Exchange, United Nations.

Paper Presented by Mr. Navin Anand on Ageing

Based on our research into older people's livelihood strategies across four countries (Bangladesh, Ethiopia, India and Tanzania), and the examples of good practice described in chapter 5, we are able to propose some key guiding principles for governments, community-based organisations, NGOs, MFIs and others working to support older people to achieve greater livelihood security.

Older people already use a range of strategies, based on sources of informal and formal support within their families and communities, to support their livelihood. But, there is a key role for government and non-government partners to provide the right kind of interventions to support all older people, recognising that older people are not a homogeneous group, and their abilities, capacities and needs vary depending on a number of factors, including their health. Evidence suggests that livelihood projects are most successful where they are tailored to older people's abilities, and, to available market opportunities, are culturally and gender appropriate, and reflect the interests of the older people involved.

Evidence also suggests that cash inputs alone, while providing vital support for older dependent people, are not the sole answer for those older people who can, and wish to, work. They need assistance in creating and diversifying their productive assets. A single-input livelihoods intervention, such as provision of animals, which fails to consider current and potential market conditions, can actually serve to increase the vulnerability of older people when emergencies arise.

Some MFIs and NGOs do offer savings and loans products that would be more suitable for older people. However, these providers would benefit from training to improve their awareness, of the role older people play as key household contributors, before microfinance can be a viable, inclusive, and replicable model of savings and loans programmes for poor older people.

The following principles and actions should promote greater involvement of older people in livelihood activities, ensuring more successful outcomes.

1. Identify livelihood options through the active participation of older people themselves. Appropriate livelihood options will depend on the social, economic, cultural and ecological environment in which older people live. Cultural and gender factors may also limit older people's ability to engage in different activities as well as physical ability and psychosocial well being, and these may not necessarily correspond to chronological age. Alternative ways to involve those who are less able - for example, through proxy labour or household labour – should be considered. Because the burden of creating a sustainable livelihood is experienced most strongly by widowed, illiterate women who are caring for other family members, it will be vital to focus on addressing the economic needs of this group, in order to ensure their livelihood security.

2. Consult older people on the development and implementation of livelihood activities. Interventions will vary according to location, the local economy and local market opportunities, as well as older people's preferences, priorities and abilities. Older people's active participation in decision-making, further ensures that the livelihood solutions developed are locally appropriate. Livelihoods activities that take older people's needs into account should be an integral component of all development and humanitarian recovery programming.

3. Involve older people in monitoring and planning. Participation is the basis for promoting the inclusion of older people. Older people must be encouraged and provided with opportunities to engage actively in community leadership, as well as in the planning, implementation, monitoring and evaluation of livelihoods programmes.

4. Support older people's associations as a mechanism for increasing older people's livelihood security. Through empowerment, information sharing, improved confidence and reduced social isolation.

5. Provide appropriate training to improve older people's fiscal literacy. Improving older people's financial skills and their confidence in managing money, can increase their uptake of formal savings and loans schemes. Careful saving and strategic lending can augment and diversify older people's asset bases, thereby, reducing economic and social vulnerability.

6. Improve older people's access to information. Inconsistent and out-of-date information on financial support services, including microfinance, government services, NGO programmes and banking options, discourages poor older people from exploring and making use of formal and informal business opportunities. It also increases older people's dependency on less scrupulous sources of credit such as pawnbrokers and moneylenders, who operate with high interest and collateral requirements. Lack of access to information is compounded by illiteracy, especially for older women.

7. Encourage MFIs and NGOs to develop age-friendly livelihood activities. Service providers need to increase their awareness of older people's needs, as both savers and, borrowers, and the crucial role that older people play in contributing to their household's resources. A variety of interventions should be supported, including revolving funds, in-kind support, and cash transfers. All lending programmes must include low interest loans, and consider flexible repayment and savings mechanisms. These should be implemented in conjunction with education and training, to enable active older people to work as well as save.

8. Advocate to government for improved representation by, and services for, older people. Pensions are critical for enhancing older people's livelihood strategies. They represent a regular income that is a vital contribution to daily living needs, supports the whole household and can also be used to invest in income-generating activities. However, most poor older people in developing countries do not have access to pensions. By lobbying governments to provide universal, non-contributory pensions to their citizens, NGOs, communities and older people themselves can ensure long-term and sustainable economic security in the form of a guaranteed, regular, minimum income. Pensions enable older people to meet their basic needs, contribute to improvements in education and health for other family members, especially children, and enable them to lead dignified, and more secure lives.

References

1. Population Division of the Department of Economic and Social Affairs of the United Nations Secretariat, *World Population Prospects: The 2008 Revision;* http://esa.un.org/unpp, accessed 13 May 2010.
2. Ministry of Social Justice and Empowerment, GOI, *National Policy on Older Persons,* New Delhi.
3. Population Division of the Department of Economic and Social Affairs of the United Nations Secretariat, *world population Ageing: 1950-2050.* (http://www.un.org/esa/population/publications/worldageing19502050/pdf/90chapteriv.pdf)
4. Heslop A and Gorman M,Chronic Poverty and Older People in the Developing World, Chronic Poverty Research Centre Working Paper no.10, 2002.
5. HelpAge India, Elders for Elders Foundation, Delhi, HelpAge India, 2007.
6. Reserve Bank of India, *Senior Citizens Savings Scheme, 2004 – Frequently Asked Questions ; http://www.rbi.org.in/scripts/FAQView.aspx?Id=62.*
7. Help Age India, *Community Self Help Groups;* http://www.helpageindiaprogramme.org/RURAL/lp_rural.html

8. Help Age International and Cordaid, *Making a living last longer - Insights into older people's livelihood strategies, 2011.*
9. National Housing Bank, *Reverse Mortgage Loan: Operational Guidelines* (http://www.nhb.org.in/RML/guidelines.php)
10. More information can be accessed from *www.upliftmutuals.org*

18

Care of the Elderly

Mathew Cherian

Introduction

Signed in 1946 and put into effect in 1948, the sweeping definition of health, in the Preamble to the Constitution of the World Health Organisation (WHO), reads, *"Health is a state of complete physical, mental and social well-being and not merely the absence of disease or infirmity"*. This definition, created in a post World War II scenario, has been questioned by some experts, who feel that it is more a definition for 'happiness' than 'health'. However, the definition widens health to the psychological and social dimension and is therefore, considered to be a good concept for health.

Health and Human Rights

The Preamble, to the Constitution of WHO also states that the enjoyment of the highest attainable standard of health is one of the fundamental rights of every human being without distinction of race, religion, political belief, economic or social condition.

Health and health care are within the rights perspective and, this is reflected in the International Covenant on Economic, Social and Cultural Rights, which India had signed on 10th July, 1979. According to *Article 12* of the

Covenant, the countries party to this Covenant, recognise the rights of everyone, to **enjoy the highest attainable standard of physical and mental health.** The steps to be taken by the countries to achieve the full realisation of this right, include the improvement of all aspects of environmental and industrial hygiene, the prevention, treatment and control of epidemic, endemic, occupational and other diseases and, the creation of conditions which would assure to all, medical service and medical attention in the event of sickness.

State of India's Older People

Although, the, country has a relatively young population, India is poised to become home to the second largest number of older persons in the world. Projection studies indicate that the number of elderly — people who are 60 years old, or more – in India will increase to 100 million in 2013, and to 198 million in 2030. This will also include a significant increase in the number of the older-old persons, i.e. persons above 80 years of age.

According to the 1991 Census, a majority of the elderly of the country, i.e. 78%, live in rural areas. This makes service delivery a challenge, especially as over 30% of them live below poverty line. Proportionately, more elderly men than women reside in rural areas, in contrast to non-elderly adult men. The latter phenomenon is due to migration of young adults to the urban areas and, the return migration of the older men, back to their native areas in the rural settings. Further, the proportion of the elderly men who live in rural areas tends to increase with age. The opposite is the case with respect to the elderly women, there is a greater concentration of elderly women, than men, in urban areas.

Current Health Status of the Elderly

Health and Wellbeing of Older Persons

The ageing process, exposes individuals to increasing risk of illness and disability. But, in developing countries, a lifetime of exposure to health problems means that many people enter old age, already suffering from chronic ill-health. Old age is often an expression of defeat and suffering; a feeling that one's biological or economic productive period of life is over. It is thereby confused with a physiological stage of life. People may feel 'old' at any age, and a lot depends on the socio-economic, health, nutritional status and other parameters of life. For example, many women in India, after years of hard physical labour, poor nutrition and many pregnancies, are on the threshold of old age, by the end of their reproductive years.

In the context of health care for the elderly in India, additional riders come into play including the ageing process that disables people undergo, in a relative and absolute manner. External negative factors are also prevalent in the country —including unaffordable health care for large majority of elders in the country — combined with poor access to, and/or poor availability of, good quality health care by the public, and low cost health systems. These create a significant gap between having the 'fundamental right' to good quality health care, and, actually being able to access such care.

For older people in the developing world, personal health consistently ranks alongside material security, as a priority concern. Physical health, for many poor people is their single most important asset, bound up with the ability to work, to function independently and, to maintain a reasonable standard of living. Illness in old age is therefore, an ever-present threat and, many older people live in fear of illness.

Despite its importance to older people, healthcare is inaccessible to many. Reasons for this include, the fact that hospitals tend to be concentrated in urban centres, far from the rural areas where the majority of older people in developing countries still live. Even those who live in cities and towns, can often only reach health facilities by using public transport, which is expensive and, in most cases, not adapted for easy access. Treatment is often unaffordable for older people, even where it is subsidised. Where fee exemption policies exist, older people do not benefit because of a lack of information, shortage of supplies and poor management. The negative attitude of healthcare providers and personnel, towards the treatment of older people, is also a powerful factor dissuading many from seeking treatment.

Older people are often excluded from public health related education campaigns, especially HIV/AIDS, TB and Vector Borne Diseases, ignoring the fact that they may be care-givers of people living with HIV/AIDS, sexually active themselves and therefore, at risk of infection or, otherwise concerned in health issues. Many Advocacy, Communication and Social Mobilisation (ACSM) campaigns tend to be youth-orientated, using language that is not relevant to older persons and ignoring the possible contribution by the elderly in facilitating public health awareness and community mobilisation.

Older people living in poverty, have little or no access to treatment, care and support services to maintain their most precious asset, i.e. their health. Even when these services are available, health and welfare professionals have little knowledge or understanding of older people's health issues. Some of the constraints are difficult to overcome, but the first step must be to ensure that older people have reliable information about what services and benefits they are entitled to, and how they can receive them in good time.

WHO estimates that, by 2020, chronic diseases, along with mental health disorders and injuries, will make up 70% of the healthcare needs, in developing and newly industrialised countries. Older people form a significant part of this caseload. If unchecked, chronic diseases might pose a serious threat to the future solvency of healthcare and social protection systems.

For the disabled, seriously ill, frail or bedridden poor older people, the family is the primary source of care - due to traditional practices as well as, due to resource limitations. However, poverty, changing family structures, migration and lack of information and support for care givers, limit the ability of the family to provide adequate care. In poor, rural and isolated communities, these services are simply non-existent. Poor older people without supportive children or spouses are completely dependent on their communities for essential and vital support, when afflicted by serious disease or other infirmity.

The challenges to the health system are twofold. The first is to postpone the onset of disease as long as possible, and, the second is to provide adequate and affordable services, if and when people develop fatal or disabling illnesses. The challenges for developing countries are particularly formidable because of the rate of population ageing, and the prevalence of absolute poverty and infectious diseases. A third and more fundamental constraint is that health expenditure in many developing countries is a tiny fraction of what is needed to meet these challenges. With rapidly growing numbers of very old people, who are most likely to require daily care, there is an urgent need to develop care and support options.

The world's elderly population is fast increasing. But there is scant information on their health needs in the developing countries. However, the information that is available indicates an urgent need towards planning for the elderly in India. The task of looking after the welfare of citizens, who are in need of physical, financial and emotional care, is a daunting one for a country where the majority of the population is barely able to live above the poverty line. One aspect of this consists, in providing affordable and adequate health care by taking into account the pathologies of old age. A second issue is the socio-economic vulnerability of the elderly — in addition to physical problems - as disease profiles are generally linked to the socio-economic status of the individual, in an economy like India.

An approach towards studying the well-being of the elderly has been, to understand their ability to be functionally competent in activities of daily living (ADL). Such an approach assesses their ability to manage routine tasks, independent of assistance from others. Significantly, the elderly living with their spouses, have a better chance of warding off disability than those without, indicating that living arrangements may have a direct as well as indirect impact on health. There are male-female and, rural-urban differences in the incidence of disability rating given to such functional competence.

Several factors determine longevity. These include heredity, scientifically constructed diet and environmental factors. Health preservation from early childhood and young age, good living conditions, physical activity, fresh air, a positive attitude and, personal hygiene play important roles in determining the duration of life. Regular health monitoring and check-ups also help to prevent disease and, thereby, prolong life.

Health Providers in India

For the last six decades, there has been a systematic, albeit inadvertent, nurturing of a largely unregulated private health sector, through neglect and mismanagement of the public health system. The lack of awareness, poor capacity building measures, inertia, apathy and the interest in achieving personal goals ahead of national ones, have all contributed to this.

Today, there are approximately 1,125,000 practitioners of different systems, registered with various medical councils in the country. Of them, only 125,000 are in government service (including those in central health services, the armed forces, railways, state insurance, etc). That leaves about a million doctors in the private sector, not to mention tens of thousands of additional,unqualified and unregistered medical practitioners. 59% of all practitioners are concentrated in cities. Similarly, 84% of hospital beds are located in urban areas. Whereas, 75 % of the population still reside in villages. This selective concentration of health care providers is a major concern to be addressed, especially since, studies have shown that those living in rural areas spend about as much on health care as those in towns.

The private health sector in India, has grown into a giant and, it is stated to be the largest private health sector in the world. With 60% - 80% of health care sought in the private sector, and households contributing 4% - 6% of their incomes, there is a whopping Rs. 400 - 600 billion private health care market, in India. Its mammoth size notwithstanding, this sector has remained almost completely unregulated.

Parts of the private sector includes, the not-for-profit charity-based NGO health sector and also, the corporate heath care sector. While the latter caters to a small, defined group of corporate employees and their dependents, the former performs a vital role in providing free or low cost health care to disadvantaged communities in the country. However, charity based health providers are often unable to sustain themselves because of increased cost of providing health care and health education, poorly thought out legislation and changes in the motivating factors that determine entry into the field of health care. Although, the charity based health care sector provides patchy, but brilliant service to some of the weaker sections of society, it is evident, that what used to be the strong backbone of the health sector at the time of independence, is now a greatly weakened and relatively insignificant contributor in the larger frame of national health needs.

Non Communicable Diseases

Non communicable diseases (NCD) are now recognised as a major cause of morbidity and mortality. The WHO Report, 2001 has indicated that NCDs account for nearly 60% of deaths and 46% of the global burden of diseases. 75% of the total deaths due to NCDs, occur in developing countries and, rapid increases have been noted and clearly linked to changes in life-style.

The prevalence of disability increases with age and, there is an urgent need to extend assistance to the elderly disabled, so that we do not overlook the well-being of one of the most vulnerable groups in our societies.

NCDs, such as cardiovascular diseases, cancer, diabetes and chronic respiratory diseases, are a cause of enormous human suffering and a threat to economies of several countries. The most prominent NCDs are linked to common risk factors, including tobacco use, alcohol abuse, unhealthy and inadequate diets, physical inactivity and environmental cancer promoting agents (carcinogens).

Many elderly, enter old age already suffering from chronic illnesses and in India, poverty, combined with difficult and inadequate access to good quality treatment, care and support for these illnesses, often implies that many of them suffer a wide range of disabilities and become dependent on family and community members.

Globally, the burden of new cases of cancer in 2000, was estimated to be 10.1 million with 56% of the estimated deaths from cancer occurring in developing countries, like India. This is projected by WHO, to dramatically increase to 20 million by 2020, with 70% of the deaths in the developing world, which has access to only 5% of the global resources. The ageing population is the single most important factor for cancer development. With the remarkable growth in its population of older people and increase in life expectancy, India's cancer problem can only be expected to become bigger than it is. Tobacco related cancers constitute over 40% of all cancers in men, while cancers of the breast, cervix and ovaries accounted for 59% of cancers in women. The Population Based Cancer Registry for the Years 2001 to 2004, reveals that in both men and women, the cumulative risk in percentage in the 0 - 74 years age group was almost double, than seen in the 0 - 64 years age group.

The crude prevalence rate for Cerebro-vascular Disease (CVD) or stroke, computed from different community surveys, is about 200 per 1 Lakh persons. Hypertension, tobacco use, obesity and diabetes mellitus are important risk factors for stroke and, the treatment, care and support of stroke victims impose an enormous economic burden on our meagre health care. According to the World Health Report 2002, CVDs will be the largest cause of death and disability in India by 2020, and about half of these deaths will occur among older people.

Cataract is the most common cause of blindness in India. Nearly 1.5% of the elderly are blind, a majority of them in the rural areas. Apart from physical disability, blindness also impinges on the mental, social and financial status of the individuals and their families. The WHO-NCPB survey in 1989, estimated that 12 million Indians were blind, and in need of eye care services.

Elderly individuals, usually face a higher risk of developing mental as well as physical morbidity. Their vulnerability to mental problems is due to several reasons, including, ageing of the brain, physical problems, socio-economic factors, cerebral pathology, emotional attitude and family structure. The biochemical and morphological changes, in the ageing brain of normal individuals are similar to those suffering from dementia. In most cases, mental illnesses coexist alongside physical problems in the elderly persons. Chronic physical disorders and sensory impairments, such as visual and hearing defects, are known to be, especially associated with mental problems of the elderly. The incidence of mental illness is strongly influenced by socio economic factors like education, economic support, whether living alone and so on. The presence of dissatisfaction with life and feelings of loneliness and self-pity, show a high correlation with mental problems. So does, the family structure and situational factors, such as a widowed status and fall in income. All these, significantly contribute to emotional problems in old age. Anxiety disorders are also common in the elderly population and, these are often accompanied by depression.

Palliative care is a human right and, should be a core-basic health service. It is fully recognised and accepted, as an essential part of the continuum of care for people living with incurable diseases like advanced Cancer, HIV/AIDS, stroke or accident related paralysis and also with other life limiting illnesses such as terminal heart, lung and kidney diseases.

By *definition*, Palliative Care is the active total care of patients and their families by a multi-professional team, at a time when the patient's disease is no longer responsive to curative treatment and, life expectancy is relatively short. Palliative care affirms life and, does not hasten death. Nor, does it prolong life. It is concerned with the quality of life as, it is important for people to live meaningfully as long as they are alive. Quality is to be determined by the individual. Quality of life therefore, relates to an individual's subjective satisfaction with life, and is influenced by all the dimensions of personhood - physical, psychological, social and spiritual. It is therefore important that people live as actively as possible, in spite of disease.

Several problems contribute to suffering. These include pain, breathlessness, nausea and vomiting, fungating wounds, anorexia, fatigue, financial burdens, social isolation, neglect, loss of social roles, sadness, depression, anger, anxiety, personality changes and changes in faith and beliefs. All of these varied problems, need to be addressed in a manner that would be beneficial to the alleviation of individual suffering as well as, to the support of those who are directly affected by the problems of the elderly individual concerned.

Many of the problems, in advanced cancer or other diseases that justify the need for palliative care, are of non-medical nature. However, health-care professionals have a very important and definite role to play. Where Palliative Care is only a means of treatment, the key points to bear in mind are patients' biological prospects, therapeutic aims and benefits, adverse effects of treatment and investigations and, the availability and affordability of options. Medical professionals therefore, need to follow 4 cardinal principles; do no harm, do good, provide autonomy to patients and do justice.

Palliative care in India, is extremely patchy and there are huge regional variations. Very few centres are currently running regular palliative care training programs. There is also the issue of non-availability of essential medicines, including oral morphine, for the relief of pain and for other symptoms suffered by those requiring palliative care. The reality in India is that most palliative care needs of people are not met and, the need for palliative care hugely exceeds supply. Even basic principles of Palliative Care are not followed in the majority of health-care institutions, including those providing tertiary care.

Apart from health-care professionals, provision for Long Term Care and Palliative Care also needs to be woven into the community fabric. The declaration of Alma Ata states that Primary Health Care is essential health care based on appropriate and acceptable methods and technology, made universally accessible to individuals and families in the community through their full participation and at a cost that the community and country can afford to maintain in the spirit of self-reliance. If implemented as desired, it would result in greater choices for patients with more information on available options and, more interactions between health care professionals and patients and their families.

Doctors and nurses need to be trained in Palliative Care, to improve their clinical skills and know-how, so that their patients are made and remain more comfortable. It would be especially good for General Physicians (GPs) to be trained in Palliative Care. GPs, geriatricians and oncologists are the main groups of doctors, who would play significant roles as Palliative Care Providers.

With a rapidly growing population, consisting presently of about 1/6 the of the global population, India has a huge impact on world health. The crude death rate in India is 8.28 per thousand people 9 million people die each year in this country. Of them, at least 60% need palliative care. At present, less than 1% of the people in India have access to palliative care.

A WHO workshop on palliative care was conducted at the Regional Cancer Center, Trivandrum, Kerala in 1993. In the early 1990s, the known Palliative Care Centres in India were Shanti Avedana Ashram, Mumbai; Pain and Palliative Care Society, Calicut (Kerala); Kidwai Memorial Institute of Oncology, Bangalore (Karnataka); GCRI, Ahmedabad (Gujarat); AHRCC, Cuttack (Orissa); BHU, Varanasi (UP); RCC, Trivandrum (Kerala), and Jeevodaya, Chennai (Tamil Nadu). Training programmes courses and workshops are held in Calicut, Chennai, Bangalore, Mumbai, Cuttack and Vellore, while regular teaching programmes or fellowships, are held in Calicut, Bangalore and Vellore.

It is very difficult, to achieve meaningful palliative care through specialist units alone. The only realistic option is the evolution of palliative care as a public health measure. To enable this, it is vital to develop dedicated and skilled manpower. In 2007, HelpAge India, along with the Indian Association of Palliative Care and the Institute of Palliative Medicine, started a project with the objectives of developing training centres for palliative care, training of health care professionals and promoting community participation and home care. The project hopes to reach out to health care providers, institutions and, to governments through advocacy and training and, to the community through awareness programmes. Since then, we have cared for 22,107 patients suffering from NCD related terminal illnesses. It is a small effort by us, but we hope to spread across India, with our sensitive caring approach.

19

Senior Citizens – The Challenge Facing Society Today

Mrs. Zena Sorabjee

A couple of years ago, we saw a shocking item in the newspapers in Mumbai. It appears that a senior citizen couple around 70 years of age, husband and wife, holding hands, jumped off the 17th floor apartment of their building.

They left behind a detailed note saying that they were taking this extreme step as they could no longer bear to stay with their son and daughter-in-law, who constantly humiliated them and mentally tortured them, in order to make them leave their flat, which actually belonged to the older couple. But, not wishing to leave their apartment and with no other recourse, they decided that life was too cruel and it was best to leave it together.

Society was shocked and, certainly made it unpleasant for the son and his wife to continue to live in that building, which they then vacated and moved somewhere else, where they were not recognized.

Apart from this incident, a film was released some years back, called 'Baghban'. This film also was a gripping portrayal of children becoming reluctant to look after their retired parents. They decided to take one parent each, and so divided the elderly couple in the winter of their lives.

Traditionally and culturally, Indians have treated elders with respect, care and compassion. The elders have usually been the most important members of the family, whose opinions and exhortations have always been taken very seriously in the guidance of the younger generation. In many cases, their decisions in matters of family, business, property, relationships, were considered as final. The young in the family, though obedient to such traditions, may have resented such customs. But, as these were age old practices, it was difficult for them to go against them.

As we entered the 20th century, knowledge of the outside world began to spread in the country. Improved communication and transport modes helped in the acquisition of knowledge and skills, and more and more of the younger generation took to western shores to secure improved education, in order to improve their material prospects. Parents and grandparents, though reluctant to send their children abroad, felt more and more that this was the only way to get better education for the children to prosper and make a mark in society.

In the country, thousands of new schools sprouted in all parts, because the government schools were not considered to have a good standard. The families would sacrifice in order to send the children to better schools. So, even if the private schools were not having high standards themselves, but because they called themselves English Medium schools, the children were sent to such below-average schools. The craze to get English education was the reason for such action. Many times, this resulted in the children becoming misfits, both in their own society and society around them. They were not fluent in English and neither, were they fluent in their own mother tongue. They therefore found it difficult to communicate in any language with fluency.

When India became independent, it proclaimed itself to be a secular State. This meant that all religions would be treated in an equal manner. Schools still taught moral science and virtues which helped form the character of the children. But, some years into independence the schools gave up teaching moral and spiritual values, which came from religious scriptures. They interpreted secularism to mean against all religions. Unfortunately, this led the children into a purely materialistic way of life leaving behind most spiritual principles.

The extended family life started breaking down. Young married couples, who may have left their village or town to move into cities for jobs, had small living space, so, they did not want their parents living with them. Besides which, the older generation found it difficult to adjust to this new way of life. And, if the parents did come to stay, they were not made welcome and treated as a burden. If the elders had no place to go back to, they had to suffer the indignity of being scolded, taunted and made to feel most unwelcome. As the children saw the manner in which the grandparents were treated, they too followed suit and like their parents, were rude and cruel with their grandparents.

The younger generation, appears to have forgotten that the grandparents have a lot to contribute towards the upbringing of the grandchildren. They are able to ingrain in the children some spiritual values, to be able to distinguish between right and wrong, make moral choices. When both parents are working, the children need wise guidance, which they will not get from an illiterate helper in the house. This wise guidance would be available with the grandparents.

Unfortunately, the institution of grandparents is dying and more and more nuclear families have become the fashion. And, as the treatment towards grandparents becomes harsh, the grandparents too, do not wish to stay with their children, if they can afford to stay separately.

So, we have these two extremes. One, where the elders hold complete sway over the family, and the other, where the elders have become dispensable and unwanted, and, treated with contempt. Where, in the past, the mother-in-law's position was supreme and to be feared, that role is now reversed and the daughter-in-law rules the roost. Both are not ideal conditions. Both situations needed kindness, compassion, love and tolerance. And these qualities are sadly lacking in family relationships these days.

One of the signs of such a breakdown is the fact that, more and more senior citizens are looking for senior citizens' homes, where they can spend the few years left of their lives. They want to enter these homes for many reasons, either they are unhappy with their families and need to find companionship with similar senior citizens, or, their children are settled abroad or in other places, and they are alone and want to be with others, having an institution to care for their daily needs.

Then, there is the case of widows, who are the most unwanted of senior citizens. Superstitious families treat such women as unlucky and, want them out of the way. Illiterate widows are taken by their children and relatives to Mathura, and abandoned at the station or on the streets.

These widows have no idea about their address or how to get back to their home. The authorities then, take them to the widows' homes in Mathura where, they eke out their lives along with other such unfortunate women.

The main causes of this deterioration in society is the absence of values in our lives. Our intellect has developed materially, but our characters have not developed spiritually.

The main emphasis, is on how to make more and more money and, to become consumers of all the attractive products that one desires to have. The "character deficit" that everyone is talking about, is what needs most to be addressed. It is very difficult to change the character of an adult who is set in his or her ways, and, who is steeped in a materialistic way of life.

Their main aim is to succeed materially in life so that, they can purchase items which will be the envy of others. Our aims are not such as to bring about the elevation of the human character. Quality education of the young is the greatest need of the day, the kind of education which lays emphasis on kindness, tolerance, compassion and unselfishness. Values need to be taught from a young age and, if these are not taught in the home, due to lack of time of the parents, then, educational institutions must take the role of the parents to bring these values in the character of the child.

The child is like a sapling which the gardener can nurture, to take any direction he wants. But, once the tree is grown, and the trunk becomes thick, it is very difficult to change its direction. The schools will have to step in to fulfil this role.

Apart from the schools, if the children are fortunate to have grandparents living with them, then that would be another source of good upbringing. The elder generation has so much experience and wisdom to share with the youngsters, it would be a pity to deprive them of this source.

I remember my old grandmother, who though never attended school, had wisdom, which she was able to share with all of us. We were fortunate to have her living with us. History was not my favourite subject, when I was young. She realized that. She would therefore, ask me to sit with her and bring my history book and, read to her. In those days, we did not refuse a grandparent. As the loud reading progressed, she would intersperse the reading with questions, which I would have to answer.

These regular readings slowly developed in me an interest in history and, that became my favourite subject. I realized, later on that it was not because she was interested in British history, which was the subject in question, but the methed she had struck upon, to make me interested and get to love the subject.

It is therefore such a pity, that we are depriving our children of the good training which the elders could give generously. Hopefully, more and more schools will take up this challenge of developing, along with the three R's, a curriculum of moral values, which will finally lead people to make moral choices, one of which would be to treat the older generation with compassion and respect.

20

Caring for the Elderly: Laws and Realities

Dr. Tahir Mahmood

Introduction

Ageing is a natural process, which inevitably occurs in the human life cycle. It brings with it a host of challenges in the life of the elderly, engineered by the natural changes in their physique and thinking. Yet the aged, in any society, constitute a precious reservoir of human resources gifted with knowledge, experience and insight. Given an appropriate opportunity, they are in a position to make significant contribution to the socio-economic development of the nation.

The population of the elderly around the world, has been increasing over the years. As per UNESCO estimates, the number of persons above sixty years of age, which was nearly 600 million in 2005, would double by 2025 and then, the world will have more elderly than young people. In India, population of the elderly was 72 million at the beginning of the current millennium and, is expected to reach $1/5^{th}$ of the country's total population by 2025.

With all the potential yet at their command, the elderly in various societies, unfortunately face multifarious problems which have been classified as follows :

(*i*) economic problems such as unemployment, income deficiency and economic insecurity;

(*ii*) physical and physiological problems such as health condition, nutritional deficiency and lack of housing; and

(*iii*) psycho-social problem such as social maladjustment, insecurity, isolation and abuse.

Elderly care emphasizes the social and personal requirements of senior citizens who need some assistance with daily activities and health care, but who desire to age with dignity. Elder care envisages fulfillment of the assisted-living needs and requirements that are unique to the elderly individuals in the society. Its parameters and modalities depend on the local cultural traditions. In the West, the elderly are seen as a heavy burden on the families and, treated as the liability of the State. Conversely, in the East, elder care is supposed to be a sacred responsibility of the younger generations. With the growing problems faced by the elderly everywhere on the globe, social and legal measures have been adopted at the national and international level.

International Concern

The situation of the elderly, was discussed by the United Nations, first in 1948 and then, in 1969 at the initiative of the Governments of Argentina and Malta, respectively. In 1971, the UN General Assembly requisitioned a comprehensive report on the problems of the elderly worldwide, together with suggested guidelines for national and international action for their solution. A World Assembly on Ageing was held in Vienna in July-August 1982 where, an 'International Plan of Action on Ageing' (IPAA) was prepared and later adopted by the UN General Assembly. Its goal was to guide the member-countries on how to deal effectively with the special concerns and needs of the elderly. The Plan aimed at promoting a fair comprehension of social, economic and cultural implications of ageing and related humanitarian issues.

In 1991, the UN adopted an 18-point programme of action for the elderly with a view to ensuring that :—

(i) all older persons have opportunity to work and determine when to leave the work force;

(ii) remain integrated in the society and participate actively in the formulation of policies which affect their well-being;

(iii) have access to healthcare, helping them to maintain optimum level of physical, mental and emotional well-being;

(iv) are able to pursue opportunities for full development of their potential and have access to educational, cultural, spiritual and recreational resources; and

(v) can live in dignity and security, and, should be free from exploitation and mental and physical abuse.

Situation in India

Religious Precepts and Traditions

All religious faiths prevailing in India, mandate youngsters to be extremely respectful to and, careful about the elderly, both in and outside the families. Sacred texts of the Hindus are replete with commands for white-hair respect and elder care. Parents and higher ascendants occupy a high pedestal, in the ancient religions of India and, especially, the mother is equated with a goddess. The same is true about Islamic teachings. The Holy Quran places parents next to God and proclaims:

> Thy Lord decrees that you worship none but Him,
> And be nice to both of your parents,
> If either of them is or both become old,
> Do not speak even a word of disrespect for them,
> And deal with them in a dignified way,

Behave with them with utmost humility,
And seek for them dignity and protection,
As they had sought for you when you were young.

[Quran : XVII : 23-24]

More than a dozen verses in different chapters of the Holy book of Islam, repeat in varying terminology the same command for deep respect and care, in favour of the parents and higher ascendants.

With the diminishing hold of religion on the people and adoption of western life styles, compliance with the religious precepts relating to the elderly, has been unfortunately declining. In view of this degeneration of values, legal and administrative measures on the part of the State for the benefit of the elderly, has become unavoidable in our country, too. On the statute book of India, there now are a number of laws which directly or indirectly afford protection to the elderly in the society.

Constitution

In India, the Constitution does not directly deal with the problems of the elderly, but its chapter on Directive Principles of State Policy, includes some provisions which have a bearing on the situation and the rights of the elderly. Article 41 mandates the State to make, within the limits of its economic capacity and development, effective provisions for securing the right to work, education and public assistance in cases of unemployment, 'old age, sickness and disablement', and in 'other cases of undeserved want'. Article 46 directs, the State to take care of interests of 'weaker sections' of the society and, protect them from social injustice and all forms of exploitation. Like all other provisions of this Chapter, these are also non-justiceable and the State is not legally bound to implement them.

Family Laws

The rights of the elderly, are mostly governed everywhere in the world by the laws of family relations. In India, we have a dual system of family law. Every community can adhere to its religion-based family and succession laws, generally known as the personal laws. We have at least four community-specific family laws in the country - (a) Hindu law (also applicable to Buddhists, Jains and Sikhs); (b) Muslim law, (c) Christian law, and (d) Parsi law – and each of these laws contain provisions which have a bearing on the rights of the elderly. Along with these laws, there is a secular family law regime which people, whatever religion they may be professing, can voluntarily adopt at the time of marriage.

The Hindu Adoption and Maintenance Act 1956, enables every male and female to adopt children in accordance with the prescribed rules. There is no upper-age limit for this purpose and so, an aged man or woman governed by Hindu law may, should he or she so desire, adopt a son or daughter. No son can however, be adopted by a person who has a son, grandson or great-grandson; and no daughter by one who already has a daughter or son's daughter - even if these descendants are living far away from, or are otherwise, neglecting the person concerned. This is a lacuna in the Act, which works to the detriment of the people.

Under the same Act, both sons and daughters are required to maintain their aged or infirm parents –including, notably, a childless step-mother – if the latter are unable to maintain themselves, out of their own income or property. Legal heirs of a deceased person, are also required to provide maintenance to the parents of the deceased, out of the property inherited by them. None of these provisions will however apply, if there is difference of religion between the person required to provide maintenance and, the one to be maintained – and this is another serious lacuna in the Act which, in this age when cross-cultural marriages are common, may sometimes pose problems for the needy elderly.

Under Muslim law too, both males and females are required to provide maintenance to their needy parents, grandparents and higher descendants. Under this law, difference of religion between the descendant obliged to provide maintenance and the ascendant required to be maintained, is immaterial. A beautiful feature of Muslim law is the rule that, while custody of children generally remains with the mother, failing her, it goes (in preference to the father) to the maternal grandmother or great-grandmother of the child. This may in certain situations, be a boon for the elderly.

The Muslim Law of Bigamy and Talaq, as applicable in India – notably, both going against the true Islamic legal principles in this regard – often plays havoc with the elderly in the community. Married women, return to their aged parents, when the husband either divorces them or brings in another wife. This becomes a burden of all sorts for the parents, causing them great mental agony and financial burden. It is generally believed that a Muslim husband, who divorces his wife, has no obligation to provide maintenance to her beyond a short period of three months. Based on an absolutely wrong understanding of Islamic law, this belief has been firmly in vogue among the Muslims of India. When the Supreme Court of India decided otherwise, in its celebrated 'Shah Bano' case decision of 1985, Muslim religious leadership tried to get its viewpoint superseded by legislation and, succeeded in securing enactment of a law called the Muslim Women (Protection of Rights on Divorce) Act 1986. Fortunately, the courts have interpreted this law in a remarkably women-friendly way, and are awarding fairly reasonable amounts of maintenance to divorced women, living with their parents or other elderly relatives. This is indeed a great relief for the elderly in the Muslim society.

The Muslim law of succession, is remarkably friendly to the aged and the elderly, both male and female. Under this law, both parents - or, in their absence grandparents or great-grandparents - of a deceased person, always get a share in that person's property. On the contrary, under Hindu law, only the mother (who is a class I heir) always inherits- the father (who is a class II heir) is not entitled to inherit in her presence, and, in the presence of a host of other class I heirs. Grandparents, both maternal and paternal, are also class II heirs, and can never get a share in the property of the deceased in the presence of any class I heir and, many other class II heirs, placed above them in the order of preference.

Under the provisions of the Indian Succession Act, 1925 too, different chapters of which apply to the Christians and Parsis, elderly ascendants have only a remote chance of getting a share in the property of their deceased ascendants.

Criminal Laws

Under the Code of Criminal Procedure 1973, parents of every person – male or female, and professing whatever religion — if they are unable to maintain themselves, can seek maintenance-orders against their sons and daughters, from the Magistrate's courts. If a son or daughter against whom such an order has been passed, fails or neglects to act on it, the Code provides the method of recovery of the maintenance amount so ordered, from him or her and also for punishment to be meted out to the defaulter by way of fine and imprisonment. The orders so passed and enforced remain applicable, until the time when a civil court decides the matter under the personal law applicable to the parties, after which the orders can be varied or withdrawn. This is supposed to be a speedy remedy for the neglected parents but unfortunately, it takes a long time to obtain it, due to the rather faulty system of administration of criminal justice prevailing in the country.

The Dowry Prohibition Act 1961 and the related provisions Code of Criminal Procedure 1973, read with the Indian Penal Code 1860, help parents and guardians of women, including the elderly among them, in dealing with the cases in which they are harassed by the husbands or in-laws of their wards, for the sake of dowry.

In appropriate cases, elderly women can seek legal relief also- under the Protection of Women from Domestic Violence Act, 2005 under which :

(a) any harm, injury to health, safety, life, limb or well-being or any other act of threatening or coercion caused by an adult member of the family causes 'domestic violence:

(b) any woman irrespective of age, who is or has been in a family relationship with others, can complain against such violence from the authorities designated in the Act. The remedies available under the Act include -protection orders, monetary relief, interim compensation, shared households, shelter homes and medical facilities.

Senior Citizens Act 2007

The most important law so far enacted by the Indian Parliament for the elderly in the society, is the Maintenance and Welfare of Parents and Senior Citizens Act 2007, which applies to all, irrespective of their religious affiliation and personal law. The remedies provided under this Act are available to :

(a) parents and grandparents (irrespective of age); and

(b) childless senior citizens (a male or female of sixty years or more).

The remedies available include:

(a) protection of life and property;

(b) medical support in hospitals established or aided by the government;

(c) placement in old age homes;

(d) punishment to those abandoning their senior-citizen relatives; and

(e) maintenance orders against sons and daughters, or grandsons and grand daughters, in case of parents, and against specified relatives, in the case of childless senior citizens.

Ground Realities

There is no dearth of aged-friendly laws in our country, as elsewhere on the globe. These may be coupled with the 1999 National Policy relating to the elderly, which requires the central and state governments to take multifarious protective and welfare measures for senior citizens. Yet, the problem remains and, needs to be attended to with greater determination.

The inter-generational joint family system prevalent in India since times immemorial, was indeed a great boon for both the aged and the young, in the families who could take abundant care of each other in all possible ways. Unfortunately, the system is fading away under the impact of modernity and, its fading away has indeed been accelerated by the modern succession laws. The traditional respect for the elderly within and outside the homes, is fast dwindling in the society. Cases of elderly abuse, both within and outside the families, are being reported in the media almost every day.

In this situation, much more is needed than just passing aged-friendly laws. An educative process to teach youngsters adequate respect for the white hair and genuine concern for the aged, is the need of the hour. All religious faiths, require their followers to be extremely kind to their aged relatives. A carefully designed curriculum, covering religious teachings regarding the elderly and legal measures for their rights, should be taught as a general course for students of all disciplines in schools and colleges. Unless social attitudes towards the elderly are disciplined, any number of laws enacted and official policies proclaimed for the benefit of the elderly, will not lead to any meaningful result.

21

Classical Dance and Ageing: The Temporal Dimension of the Body

Guru Shovana Narayan

'Dance is a poem in which each movement is a word', said Mata Hari. In the recitation of such a special 'poem', the dancer's manner of delivery affects the mood, fragrance, meaning and interpretation of each movement of the 'poem'. A delicate balance between beauty and perfection, however, it is not only the attitude and personality of the dancer but also the physical prowess that lends itself to delineation and interpretation.

Physical prowess and ageing therefore, are incompatible. But ageing is a natural phenomenon and a harsh reality. In the world of classical dance, the respected treatise 'Abhinaya Darpana' essays that, a dancer should be young, full breasted, graceful, supple and slim. Virtuosity in rhythmic aspect of dance, therefore, becomes inherent in the delineation of 'nritta' (technical virtuosity) arm of dance that includes, acrobatic features. Herein, it is the suppleness of youth that allows execution of various kinds of 'bhramaris' (pirouettes) and 'utplavanas' (jumps), as well as the dexterity and speed in the execution of footwork with demanding clarity and agility. Even, though Indian classical dance is dressed up in themes and narratives, yet virtuosity in dance is indeed the attractive pillar. 'Nritta', a celebration of the 'aesthetics of the difficult', is possible by certainly not the aged. If youth is a crucial aspect of the dance scenario, then what are the options for an ageing dancer?

Dance however, is not 'nritta' alone. It also includes 'nritya' (emotional and mimetic) and 'natya' (dramatic), laying emphasis on grace with rigorous emotional demands. Living dance is required for reaching the soul and elevating oneself. Herein, it is layers of experience that provides the catalyst in the fermenting process of maturity and internalisation, key factors for dance. Vibrancy of youth is just one of the steps in this 'marinating' process. The internalisation of dance, when the identities of dance and dancer merge to form one whole, comes only with experience.

On the artistic front, ageing or 'mature' or 'senior' dancers bring with them, loads of experience. Economy of movements in a rhythmic pattern, 'tora' or 'paran', or a slight quirk of the wrist in the 'thaat ang' for example, speaks as much as the volley of movements performed by the young. In the delineation of 'abhinaya', colouring the emotional canvas with depth and varied hues, is sought to be done by the experienced yet ageing dancer with economy of movements that is at once so rich in vibrancy of emotions. One cannot forget the examples of aged Balasaraswati performing 'Krishna nee Begane Baro', and, of the elderly Shambhu Maharaj essaying 'abhinaya' to 'Kaun Gali Gayo Shyam', that touched the hearts of the audience.

The harsh reality of ageing is not devoid of inherent dichotomy. Even while feting senior and experienced dancers, there are very few festivals and occasions when such senior artistes are sent as representatives of Indian culture. Usually, the balance is in favour of the young and talented dancers. This is understandable as the young are more presentable and supple. Even so, the canvas is dotted with admittedly a few examples as that of Guru Kelucharan Mohapatra, Pt Birju Maharaj and Sitara Devi, that have defied age.

Even with waning of physical stamina, agility and endurance that inevitably accompanies the physical ageing process, the desire to remain in active performing life does not decline. While recognising the emotional and physical pain suffered by such senior artistes, it is tragic if such senior artistes try to be half their age by being stubbornly obtuse to the ageing process. Hence, re-addressing and re-masking of ageing process, through newer understanding of the body capabilities and addressing the inevitable psycho-scarring process that accompanies ageing, become key factors for the ageing dancers. More often than not, the experienced have shown grace in chalking out a new path and identity for themselves and their dance. Many find new roles in teaching, imparting knowledge and nurturing young talents or applying their experience in new creative choreographic works. Here too, the scene is not free from prejudices. Once again, steel determination, belief in one's work and a steadfast approach, is required of the 'senior' dancers. Realizing that the frontiers of dance can never be static and without breaking away from tradition, innovation and creativity are brought to the fore by the intelligent 'senior' dancers. This has kept them in public demand, in their new 'avatar'.

On the economic front, the insecurity of dancers, young and old, is a major issue. Engulfed in an age where market forces of commercialization sets the pace, despite the extraordinary talent and long hours per day of 'sadhana' behind them, recognition and success comes painfully slow to the world of classical dance. In such a situation, when the young classical artistes are struggling to make ends meet, the position of the ageing dancer is not rosy. Not only the necessity of income to support oneself and one's family, ageing is also accompanied by health problems and various family issues. Income for a dancer is related to performances. With increasing age, the income starts dwindling due to lesser number of performances, barring those few cases of senior ageing artistes whose works are highlighted and celebrated through intelligent somatic practice.

Even in the much acclaimed rosy picture of kingdoms of yore, when the artistes received royal patronage and were entitled to pension when past their prime, such as in the case of 'guni jan khanas' of various kingdoms of Rajasthan, the situation is very different today. It is during their prime that the dancers have to make provisions for rainy days. Government patronage extends to giving grants to various institutions in terms of salary and performance grants spreading thin their limited resources. Thus, the luxury of a steady income, much needed pension and medical insurance is unknown to most of the dancers, barring the artistes employed in the constituent dance institutions under the Sangeet Natak Akademi. Even in such institutions, retirement age has always been an issue, leading to discussions whether such a bureaucratic criterion is applicable in the field of creativity such as dance, when the best comes with age and experience.

Matters are even more serious in case of dancers who suffer health problems or become subject to injury, when in the prime of their dancing career. Income to support themselves and their family even at the young age, let alone in old age, is a serious issue where help and support in terms of insurance or pension are not forthcoming. In this competitive scenario, it is a 'do and die' situation. While the Sangeet Natak Akademi has a scheme of meagre pension and insurance support, but these are largely applicable to SNA awardees, leaving the large mass of artistes to fend for themselves.

Place to stay and place to practice, have always been an issue for classical dancers, young and old. Mounting rents, coupled with a disinclination of landlords to rent out premises to dancers that is partly grounded in age old prejudices, have added to the insecurity of artistes. All their earnings even during their prime, have not been adequate for purchase of flats by many. Thus, there has been a tendency to bank upon the scheme of the central govt. for government allotment. But, this comes at a price of uncertainty as eviction notices are served by the Ministry of Urban Development on completion of the required time period of allotment. How often, cases of elderly 'senior' artistes pleading with the government for extending their period of stay have come to light ! Arguments put forth by some functionaries in government and public life include that, government allotments are not eternal and that, during the period of govt. allotment, the artistes should have made necessary arrangements for his or her permanent stay. True. But, with the extraordinary spiralling prices, no classical artiste can afford to do so, especially an ageing dancer.

The woes of dancers do not end here. Unable to practice in their apartments, as the sound of dance practice accompanied by thumping of feet and ghunghuroos disturb the neighbourhood, the dancers have to rent places for their practice. But, the situation here too, is grim. In certain places like Delhi, while use of basements are allowed for practice of lawyers, chartered accountants and such other categories, for some inexplicable reason, dancers have been excluded from the list. Furthermore, the very few places available are beyond their means. Hence, an ageing dancer who wishes to sustain himself and his family, through imparting knowledge of dance to the interested younger generations of today, is unable to do so.

Faced with such uncertainties, it is distressing to find that progenies of hereditary artistes, are embracing other more lucrative forms of art. With this increasing trend, it is feared that some of our traditional arts would be lost forever. One glaring example is that of lost heritage of Kathak dance practice in a village, founded over 900 years ago and which still goes by the name of Kathak Bigha at Amas, Gaya, Bihar. The village has some 50 to 60 houses, once thriving with Kathaks but now depleted, as they have all migrated due to lack of patronage here. According to locals here (the new inhabitants of the Kathak Village), these Kathaks had been pursuing dance and music as careers, performing in and around the Surya and Shiva temples. Late Pt. Kanhaiya Mallik himself, traced his family tree and the practice of Kathak from the time of the Saạm Veda. He also stated that according to his ancestors, the Kathaks had been living in this Kathak village for almost a thousand years. His grandson also spoke of the ancient family tradition of Kathaks, but which he himself is not pursuing because of lack of patronage, similar to that of his father who is a clerk in the Forest Department.

Yet while this is true, it is equally noteworthy that new practitioners of dance are coming from non-hereditary families. Had it not been for figures such as Rukmini Devi Arundale and Madame Menaka, the dance scenario would have been very different today. It was Rukmini Devi, as the first Brahmin girl from an elite family who took to the traditional dance of the devadasis, the dasiattam, and along with the support of E. Krishna Iyer and Raghavan, revamped and re-christened 'dasiattam' to Bharatanatyam, thus imparting respectability and resuscitation to an art form that was being thrown away by the Anti-Devadasi legislations that had received overwhelming support from members of the devadasi community. In one stroke, she not only provided security and new lease of life to several members of the dancing community, especially the aged and experienced gurus, but also gave new India a chance to claim her rich cultural heritage. This newly created dance was claimed to be ancient by a 'backward projection' in time. 'A dance was created in the past in order to be restored for the present and future', said Schechner and Mohan Khokhar. Madame Menaka, on the other hand, enlarged the ambit of Kathak performers to include women from respectable families, which till hitherto had only the traditional male Brahmin Kathaks as the keepers of this ancient dance form. As borne out by the 4th century BC Prakrit inscription (pre-dating the Natyashastra) and later, by census records of William Crooke, James Princep and Buchanan in the 19th century and the records of Munshi Bhagwandas Tehsildar, Allahabad (19th century), to an enquiry conducted about the caste of Kathaks, it emerged that the traditional Kathaks largely belonged to Kanyakubj Brahmin and Gaur Brahmin fraternities.

It is surely a dichotomous situation. In the twentieth century, in the wake of cultural and social renaissance, when traditional classical arts were recognised as the basis of our rich cultural heritage, yet even in the twenty first century, classical dancers have a tough fight for their day-to-day existence and sustenance, which becomes more acute in their old age, in spite of dance space creatively allowing and accommodating ageing process. But, it is their indomitable spirit that still propels them to serve in total dedication, the world of spirituality and harmony through classical arts, nurturing and preserving our rich cultural heritage in spite of all odds. The government has certain schemes in place, but these are just drops in the ocean. Much more is needed to be done. Today, when the impact of soft power is becoming more and more visible and when there is a new form of emerging identity crisis in the wake of fast paced globalisation and commercialisation, it is necessary that steps are taken to address the problem at its very roots. A compulsory subject could be introduced in schools, from primary stage onwards, relating to an appreciation of the history, philosophy and contribution of the field of performing arts, in all related spheres such as trade and economics, architecture, sculpture, painting, growth of literature, environment etc. so that, it benefits every individual in the society by understanding the inter-relevance of all spheres of activity. A contributory pension scheme could be introduced for the performing artistes. A health insurance scheme could be introduced for the performing artistes, as has been done in the Central Sangeet Natak Akademi for the awardees. Special incentives could be introduced for the media for better and wider coverage of 'traditional classical' performing arts, in order to create an encouraging environment for the classical arts. Facilities of rehearsal halls could be provided at nominal rates. Special quota at cost price could be provided for classical performing artistes in various government housing schemes such as DDA housing schemes. Special provisions are required, for allowing classical performing artistes to be able to rent basements for their practice as well as for renting out portion of their institutions, to help support the running and maintenance cost.

Perhaps, some beginning could be made by some of the corporate houses and initiatives taken to address few key issues under their 'corporate social responsibility'. Special incentives in terms of tax benefits could be introduced for making sponsors allocate and spend at least one-third, if not fifty percent, of the money spent annually on sponsorships, for promoting traditional classical performing art events and for taking steps to address issues relating to the nurturing of classical performing arts and artistes, especially the experienced elderly.

It is not too late to recognise the need for cultural preservation, and while making efforts of addressing issues of dance and ageing dancers, society would be helping itself in not loosing the basis of our very 'being'.

But, even with all pains of ageing and of insecurity, Martha Graham is so true when she sums it up by saying : 'Dance is the language of the soul. It is a song of the body; either of joy or pain.'

22

Aged the Untapped Resource of the Nation

Dr. Padma Seth

In his monumental work, "Ageless Body and Timeless mind", the great healer, Dr. Deepak Chopra writes, "elevation of the youth as the ideal of life, is oneside of the coin, the other is the denial that old age exists" Ageing as per the healer is much more of a choice, than people ever dream. But the longer a person lives, is often looked at in our country that threatens debility, disease, pain, decay and dependence. But in other cultures, long life represents a joy and old age is considered a blessing. Every added year draws more value and respect. Elaborating this phenomena, Dr. Chopra talks of a legendary artist of Japan by name Hokusai,who was proficient as a Woodblock artist from his younger days. But he was apparently not satisfied with his performance and skill in drawing. However he is expressed hope that at his age of 70 or 80, he is expected to possess the best of skills and at the age of 100, he hoped that his art would become more sublime and at 110 years of age, he will reach utmost bliss. The artist was unmindful of the results of ageing and of natures truth, that his life would be snapped anytime by death and that his skill would have no future. He was said to have died at the ripe age of 90 years.

A Country has its "Problems and Values"

Every country has its own problems and value systems. For instance, combating environmental degradation, pollution, drugs, disease, corruption, discrimination on the basis of sex, caste, creed and religion, superstition and customary practices, security threats to individuals and the society as a whole besides, a country facing acute crunch in resources both economic and skilled manpower etc. A nation if it often fails to and even ignores exploitation of women and children, the flourishing sex-trade, trafficking at large, the ever increasing number of widows discarded by their families to destitution, and humiliated by archaic customs and practices, the unquenchable poverty of the masses, ignorance and unbending attitudes and added to these, the government's uneconomic spending on superfluous concerns, it should be ashamed of, when its poor citizens queue up for a marsel of food before charities, temples, masjids and churches. However, solutions have to be found.

Growing Number of Aged and Retired

Our government has put a moratorium on the working-age of employees, including professionals, scientists, administrators, managers, teachers, doctors and a host of others in various fields. The government and institutions both public and private absolve themselves of their liabilities once they retire. Those entitled to pensions do receive half of their salaries as pension and many others go without the benefits. The retired hardly matter to the working of the government and other institutions. Suddenly descending from the status of a government employee to exclusion from the service, the retired feel a big void in their lives. They feel ignored and command very little or no respect in society.

Though India has a large volume of youth, the aged are growing in numbers too. The skilled, educated professionals, though alert do miss their working life and routine discipline after retirement. Most of Indians hail from joint family backgrounds, where they have learnt to work as a team in an environment of comraderi. In emergencies and other times, each of the family member feels the responsibility to attend to the common tasks of the household. This culture that they have imbibed from their younger age lasts for ever, until their physique refuses to co-operate to perform. Irrespective of growing age, like lawyers, self-employed ones, independent entrepreneurs, artists, even politicians merrily carry on their work outside the restrictive rules of government that do not bind them.

Legendary Aged – Ageless and their Zeal

Most of the older persons, whether at home or in pblic life, have demonstrated their zeal to continue to work. Age has never curtailed their enthusiasm or talent nor skill. Sarojini Naidu thundered the British at the Round Table Conference demanding swaraj with Gandhiji. Thousands, unmindful of their age or status barged into the freedom struggle Dr. Muthulakshmi Reddy, a medical doctor fought against trafficking of women and girls and started the Avvai home for the destitute women and children. She was unmindful of her duties as a legislator in the Madras assembly, started the very first Cancer hospital. Dr. Durgabai Deshmukh, a stalwart Social worker, a freddom fighter, after doning the mantle of a member of Parliament. Member of the Planning Commission, Chairperson of the Central Social Welfare Board, spent all her life designing strategies to help women and children's education, their safety, upkeep and rehabilitation. With her single devotion and purpose, she created monumental institutions like the

Andhra Mahila Sabha both at Madras and Hyderabad and various districts around and a host of hospitals, tourist centres, institutions like Indian Council for social development, the Population council, the Andhra Education society, Blind Relief Association, orthopaedic hospital for the handi-capped, printing press, etc. Both governmental and non-governmental organizations are still debating on the same issues she fought for and solutions long ago. At the age of seventy, when her eye sight was fast receding she took to oral language and got recorded the various milestones that she crossed. A galaxy of women academicians, scientists, poets, craft persons found their mentors in Dr. Rajkumar and Amrit Kaur, an associate of Gandhiji and a medico, gave up her royal luxuries and plunged into the service of the nation. Her relentless work for the weavers and fisher women and got them their visibility as contributors to development. She also created the Lady Irwin college for Home Science for girls. If not for her initiative with the help of Dr. Durgabai Deshmukh as member of the Planning Commission, the All India Institute of Medical Sciences would not been established. These legendary women have sacrificed their self interest for the wellbeing of the country and its people. Their age has not deterred them from their noble pursuits. At their lowest ebb, the craft persons of this land were almost sent into oblivion in the British days, It was after independent India, Dr. Kamala Devi Chattopadhyaya extensively travelled villages far and wide in our country and encouraged them and actively assisted them with the craft councils she started under the National and State Crafts Boards. These, doyens each and every one of them were institutions in themselves and were visionaries. Smt. Lakshmi Menon and Smt. Aruna Asaf Ali's contributions were no less. While the former not only served the country as a minister of external affairs, she unstintingly pledged hers and her meager savings from the Bank to purchase land for the premier women's organization i.e. the All India Womens Conference. Her unassuming personality and her experience and wisdom in sharing with the country and its women has no rival. Aruna Asaf Ali, a star of the QUIT India movement, a revolutionary worker for the upliftment of the labour force and a true messiah for the working class, was a great support to the Trade Union movement in the country.

Have any one of them got worried about their personal health ? Their history sheets Only show their passion for service and performance. They refused to even think about their old age or any accompanying disability. How can arts, music and dance be left without a mentor. Dr. Rukmini Arundale, a theosophist and an avid connoseur of music dance and drama, a true patriot as her earlier legendary contemporary sisters created a monumental institution i.e. Kalakshetra at Chennai, that has a global following. Not only she helped in resurrecting the classical arts of music, dance and drama, she made the world understand the richness of Indian classical disciplines. Not merely all aforesaid luminaries, all could fulfill the aspirations of their brothers and sisters, but unequivocally fought for equality and eqlui justice. Land mark legislations starting from the Hindu Code Bill, the various legislations abolition of child marriages, widow remarriage, women's equal rights in property and wages, right to health and education, prohibition are their stellar contribution, that we owe to them for generations to come.

Work Ethics of the Aged — Unrecognised

In India and world over, progress and development are measured by the performance and implementation of the policies and programmes of the government and public undertakings and institutions. The world of corporates remain comparatively free except for limitations, monetary and fiscal imposed on them by the government of the day. Even the Five Year Plans, we find are unmet fully and the commitments made, spill over to the next Five Year Plans. In the fast changing world of technology, even minds are running fast and impatient and do not care to attend to details unlike meticulously done, in the days of yore. Values have somersaulted following alien global standards. This is believed to be the culture of today. The painstaking work ethics of the older people are not valued leave alone recognized.

At a time when education of every child is not only a fundamental right, the Right to Education (RTE) has made it mandatory for every child upto the age of 14 years to go to school and obtain the basic education. Even for imparting the early education to children, the infrastructure by way of schools and of teachers is far below the requirement. This is a huge responsibility to attend to a humanity of children. The new recruits as teachers, most of them not fully qualified or trained, lack the aptitude nor commitment to pursue teaching children that too in remote villages. They fail to realize this responsibility as their duty. In todays work culture, moving and shifting from job to job is regarded as a value. This is why the children attending schools are not able to establish a rapport with the fast changing teacher community. The emotional and the human touch most needed for small children to develop with their teachers is lost. The consequent lack of respect shown to teachers as a community is dwindling fast. Past bonding with earlier gurus/teachers is obviously evaporating into thin air. Therefore the impatient youth of today, has no time to show irrelevant courtesies to the teachers and the luxury of wasting time on them and their feelings and dictates.

Today more than ever the country needs knowledge and services of their aged to rejuvenate and infuse faith and confidence into the despondent youth who are confused in the fast changing ethics of today. Shortsightedness of the younger generation needs to be corrected, by the experienced and pragmatic visions of the aged, whose expertise can help and assist the governmental commitment in implementing their plans and programmes. This can save the national exchequer from spending largesses on foreign trained experts for various fields of study.

Aged: The Knowledge- and Treasure

It is not to hold a brief for the aged, it is time we realize that losing their knowledge, we are foregoing the country's treasure. The knowledge and experience of generations, called out of hard work and sincere pursuit cannot be given a miss.

Our national economy is far from being robust and our government's commitment to education and health policies remain unfulfilled for want of good educators, committed complement of doctors, nurses and the auxiliary forces in all areas of study and work. Added to this, there is no National Policy for the aged except to look at them as recipients of doles. The aged can act as a Subsidiary Force to manage the requirements of the RTE and the needed medical hands. There are no innovative strategies developed to utilize the skills and services of the aged. Governmental parameters of branding people attaining a certain age as non-productive sounds a death knell to the whole country's progress. The economy of a nation depends on its human resource. It sounds like a crime to let their knowledge and skills unheeded and castaway. It is most economical, to seek their time and knowledge to let the aged fill the void, where there are no recruits. The retired and the aged may not expect scales of pay and perks. They will be satisfied and willing to help with minimum logistical support and honour.

Role of Aged in Labour Intensive Economy

A functioning economy is based on reliable information and on reports that can be trusted. Experienced persons, capable of taking decisions are not merly pushing exercises. Unlike in the West that is capital intensive economy, ours remains to be labour intensive. Hence man-woman power is what is needed to be deployed in numerous areas of development. The capital intensive approach is not viable for India, in areas of knowledge and services, where cost effective ways of engaging the old and the aged need immediate attention. "The learning society", as Peter Drucker said. "is taking over capital intensive societies too. Innovation and Entrepreneurship are looking at change as an opportunity, where there will be no problems of social acceptance."

Aged Can Save and Accelerate Development

Critical areas like conservation of natural resources, recycling waste, saving environment and ecology, introducing renewable sources of energy and devising strategic models to bridge the hiatus between rural and urban belts are far beyond officialdom to tackle with bureaucratic approaches. The aged and the experienced have a big role to play in numerous areas where government cannot tread. Besides, educated professionals, even skilled farmers, agriculturists, flori culturists veterinarians, who have the experience and expertise in working in the field have their ground knowledge to share. What engineers and doctors deliberate on issues for years, skilled workers like the automobile mechanic, better if he is aged and experienced, can understand the pulse of the motor car than the thermo dynamic experts. Specially in the field of agriculture and cultivation, most of the educated girls specially meant to be extension service providers and workers hardly ever visit the fields to understand, to advise and to counsel the farmers in the processes of production. Even gene specialists and agriculturists recognize the native knowledge of the farmers who are in close touch with the processes growing and nurturing the seeds wheat, rice, etc. and pulses, as also vegetables and fruit cultivation. Knowledge is for sharing and not for hoarding. Who can be better equipped than the tolerant old professionals and specialists ? Also after harvesting the fathers know how to save their produce both in sun and rain. Alas, the officials draw up building godowns for conserving the produce. Still for the past few years, volumes of tons of rice and wheat were let lie unattended and so much so got spoilt that was not useable even by the cattle. Poor people wait on the one side while the food grains get wasted unstored.

Today much money is spent on infrastructure, transportation, vehicles for both road and railway traffic, on variety of vehicles, the building campuses not maintained. This public property costs the government scores of funds and they are left like orphaned assets of the country. We need vigilant eyes and ears to save the properties of the nation. IB intelligence specialists, retired officials of the RAW and of thousands and lakhs of personnel retired, are left to count their days to languish in isolation and exclusion. Our ancient system of teaching and learning in the guru shishya parampara and of the old physicians trained in indigenous medicinal systems are looked at inferior. After many decades, our government has changed its stance though partially to look at alternative medicinal systems which are totally cost effective and are still practiced in the rural areas spread all over the country.

The security systems like the police of various brands mostly start action after the crime is reported, more than being preventive. This is not to decry their very presence is looked at as a deterrent to criminals at large. Lack of legal awareness and apprehensions amongst the public about the genuineness of the police and the prevailing corruption, violence can be reduced and an environment of awareness can be ushered by lawyers, teachers, public personalities, etc.

Just making and pronouncing a number of policies cannot absolve governments of their duty and responsibility. It is high time for the Planning Commission and Ministries, Departments of Government to rethink creatively to realize the vast human force of the aged lying unutilized and unrecognized and they are the solution to the numerous malaise faced by nation's governance.

The National Rural Health Mission for instance has started health centres at three levels, at the district, at the block and at the village levels. The infrastructure by way of building may be welcome, but the equipment and the personnel provided are inadequate. The doctors are loaded with work of visiting many villages so also the village level nurses, who can hardly be in one village one day in a month and the doctor visits once in three months. There are anganwadis, the panchayati raj system in place and a school without facilities and a bath room for girls. RTE gets to be infructuous. These analysis form the basis to recommend to the government that by using aged educators, professionals and even skilled personnel much of the unimplemented areas and policies can be covered.

The simple rural folk who are living a hard life struggling to eke out a living often seek collecxtive betterment for their village unlike the urbanites who are only interested in their self and individual gains. Public health issues, drinking water needs of the village and hygiene and sanitation still are the neglected areas needing immediate attention. These service areas can easily absorb a large number of the aged intelligentsia, though bureaucracy has its own misgivings. What is needed is deep commitment to pursue to understand the problems and find solutions and not treat anywork as below the dignity. A common issue of construction of latrines for the underprivileged in villages, financed by the government stops half way. Once we explore the why of it, either corrupt contractors understand the sabotage the work or the villagers do not understand the need for the same, or they do not want to change their sanitary habits, or tardy disbursement of funds midway. If this issue has to be sorted, we need unbiased persons who have the experience of tapping the government and plan with the villagers to start work when the resources are ready, or when villagers themselves can offer their services in the construction of the same. Even non-governmental bodies work more in the urban areas and dread to go to the villages where life is hard devoid of comforts. By engaging willing and experienced aged persons, much of the time wasted on such issues of day to day life can be eased out.

"We need tireless energy and courage.........these virtues can only be if there burns the flame of passionate love of humanity" said Dr. Rajkumari Amrit Kaur, who proudly envisioned the AIIMS for Delhi. As per recent reportage in the Times of India Newspaper dated the 27th April 2012 on the staff crunch at the AIIMS Says:

"Which sees a footfall of 10,000 patients a day to attend the OPD alone, is crippled by an acute shortage of manpower. The Associate Professors 16 and Nursing lecturers 13 are lying empty." Likewisw lakhs of primary teachers posts are lying vacant in villages in a number of States. Why the government announces and publicises through the various media, if it has neither proper plans and time schedules for such needed appointments of staff or if they have yet to commit resources for the same. The reasons may be many for these lapses but only those people, who have time to spare and who possess knowledge to understand the various ifs and buts in hospital and school management and bureaucracy, alone can save the situation.

Aged an Invaluable Asset

These are critical times, when we need flexible and pragmatic strategies to combat the ills, lacunae in implementation of policies and programmes of the Government of India and of the States. A humane understanding of the aged and their capabilities to intervene in areas unable to be handled by government and also to develop policies, is needed. It is urgent to extend a helping hand to the aged, who will be only too willing to offer their assistance in speeding development. More than ever before, the truth of the ancient saying , "that those who are without a vision will perish whether it be an individual or an institution." After all, the Aged are not step children of the democratic nation. The able and the aged are an invaluable asset, while the disabled are the nations responsibility. They all need attention and understanding.

Summing up the causes for the tardy state of affairs in the early days of the Indian Republic, Dr. Rajkumari Amrit Kaur, the very first Minister of Health government of India, just a week before her demise, she wrote to the members of YWCA," "Although finance is very necessary, because economic security means more self reliance. I am not really perturbed about raising funds as I Am about the paucity of first class personnel. For, no good work ever languished for wants of funds but lack of dedicated workers" Such were the stalwarts of yester years who had only the good of humanity in their hearts.

23

Nutritional Status of the Elderly

Mathew Cherian

India invested in health care as a method of improving the human resources so that they can contribute effectively to national development. As a result of interventions to improve health and nutritional status of the citizens, the life expectancy of Indians has doubled from mere 33 years in 1950 to over 66 years by the turn of the century and is expected to reach 72.5 year by 2026. The population of elderly has been projected to double from 6.4% to 12.4 % by 2026 (Figure 1)[1]

Figure-1 Percentage of population by broad age-groups: India 2001-2026

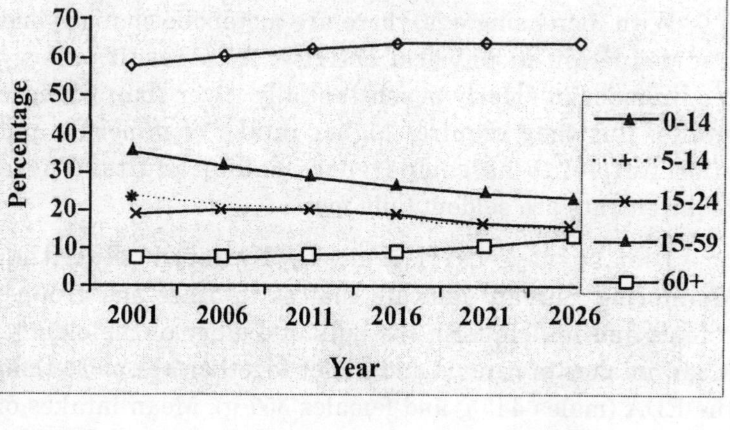

The number of women and men in the age groups 60->80 in 2001 and in 2011 is given in Table 11. Currently vast majority of the elderly are in their sixties, are likely to be active and healthy; with essential health and nutrition care they can continue to be productive and contribute to the improvement in quality of life of the family and the country. Relatively very few are in their eighties – when they might require major support system. Among the elderly belonging to all the age groups women out number men. Majority of them have been housewives and depend on their family have to take necessary steps to improve or atleast prevent deterioration in quality of life of these women who had toiled for the family all thorough their life.

Age-group	*2001*			*2006*			*2011*		
	Persons	*Males*	*Females*	*Persons*	*Males*	*Females*	*Persons*	*Male*	*Female*
60-64	25692	12592	13099	27442	13724	13718	32405	16693	15712
65-69	20514	10043	10471	22506	10813	11693	24397	11991	12406
70-74	15996	7950	8046	16860	8065	8795	18944	8909	10034
75-79	5309	2832	2476	12012	5794	6217	13092	6075	7017
80+	3176	1525	1651	4760	2350	2411	9632	4470	5163

Dietary Intake of the Elderly

With increasing age, there are metabolic changes and also reduction in physical activity. As a result, energy requirement in elderly is substantially lower than younger adults. But they require higher intake of minerals and micronutrients as compared to young adults. These requirements are seldom fully met.

Diet surveys carried out by National Nutrition Monitoring Bureau[2] indicate that as in other age groups, cereals and millets form the bulk of dietary of the elderly. Mean intakes of cereals and millet together are more than the RDA (males 445 g and females 357 g). Mean intakes of pulses are low both in males and females (31 g and 27 g respectively). The dietary intake of pulses and green leafy vegetables was less than RDI in all age groups in both sexes. Intake of other vegetables, though better than green leafy vegetables was still lower than the RDI in both sexes (Figure 2). Elderly individuals also face problems in ensuring appropriate dietary intake because of alteration in taste with increasing age and loss of teeth.

Figure 2 Mean daily intake of foods

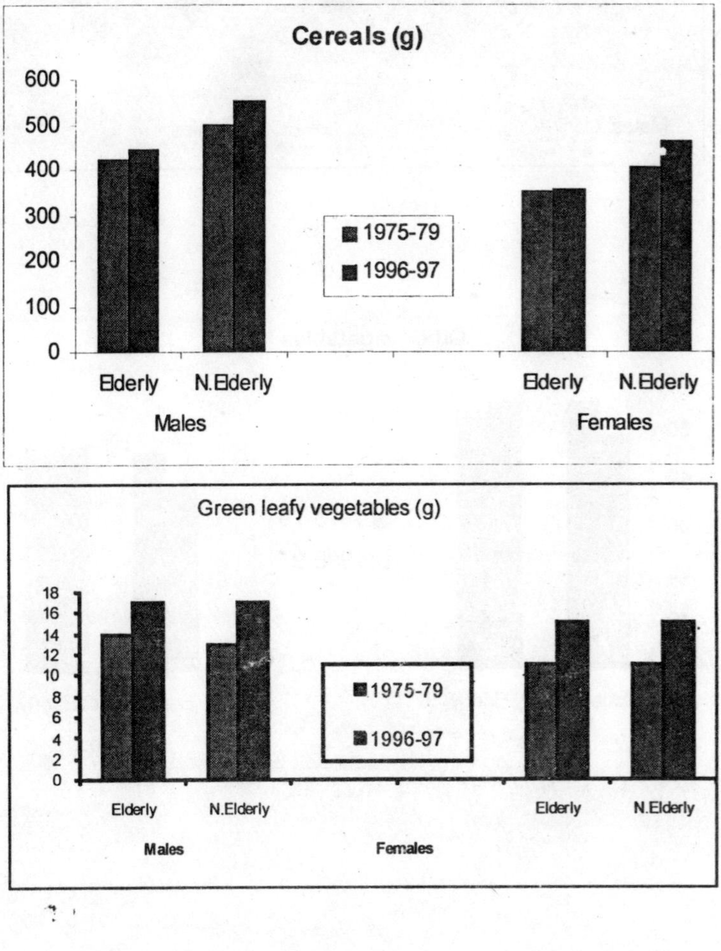

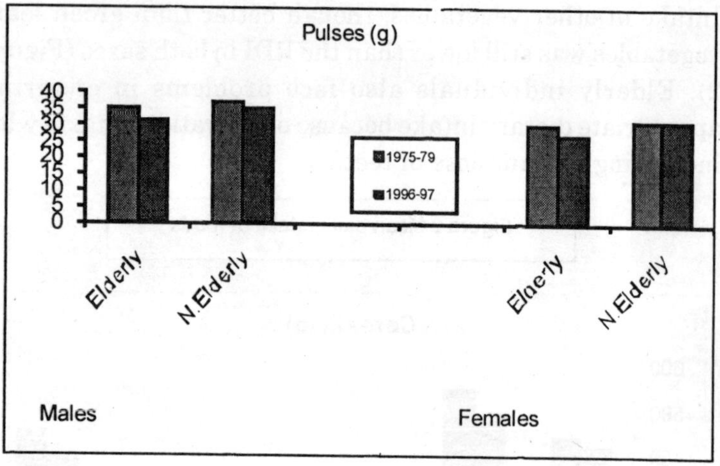
Pulses (g)
40
35
30
25
20
15
10
5
0
1975-79
1996-97
Elderly
N.Elderly
Elderly
N.Elderly
Males
Females

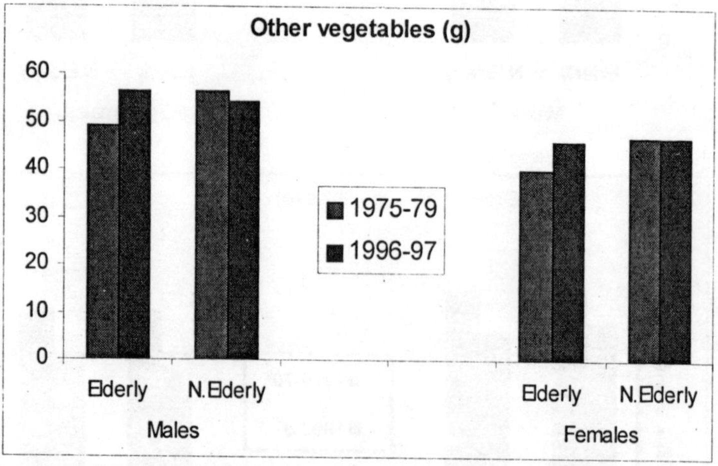
Other vegetables (g)
60
50
40
30
20
10
0
1975-79
1996-97
Elderly
N.Elderly
Elderly
N.Elderly
Males
Females

Figure 3: Mean daily intake of nutrients

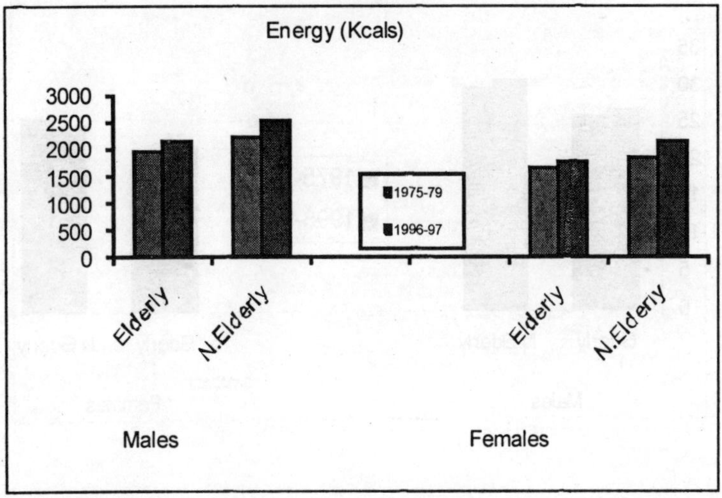

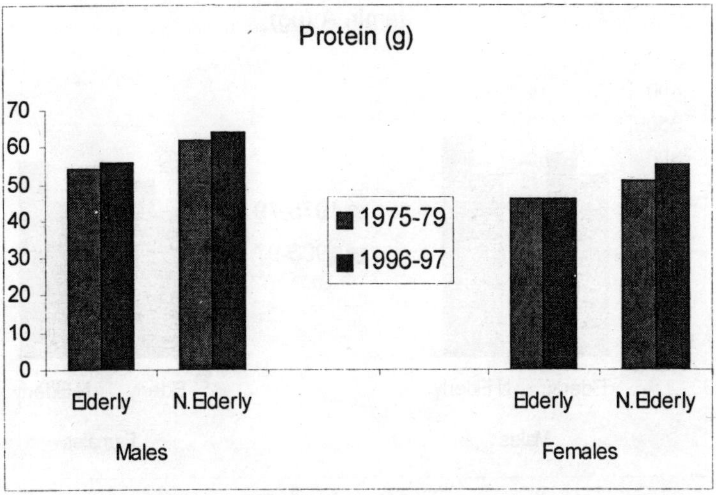

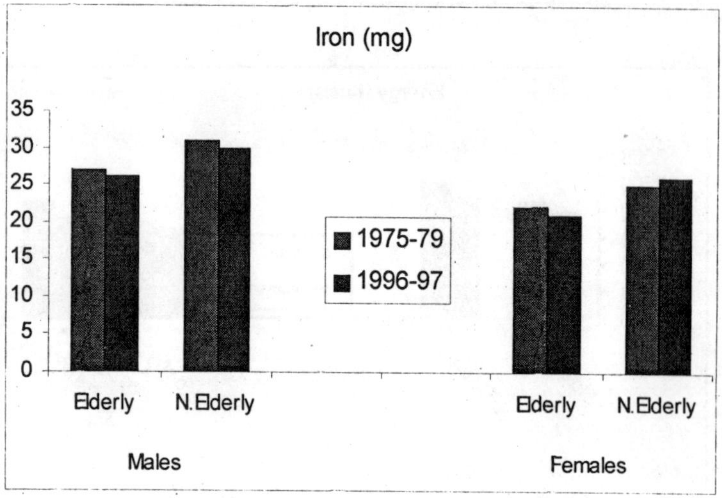
Iron (mg)
35
30
25
20
15
10
5
0
1975-79
1996-97
Elderly
N.Elderly
Elderly
N.Elderly
Males
Females

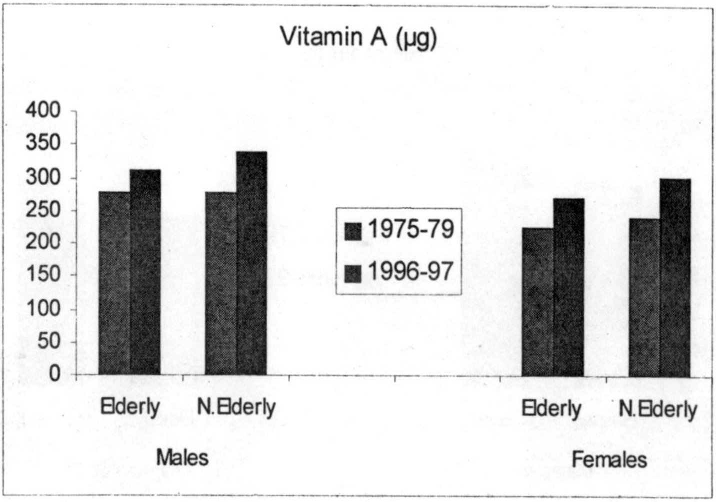
Vitamin A (μg)
400
350
300
250
200
150
100
50
0
1975-79
1996-97
Elderly
N.Elderly
Elderly
N.Elderly
Males
Females

The mean and median intakes of nutrients by elderly men and women are presented in Figure. 3. The mean intake of protein was slightly less than the Recommended Dietary Intakes in both the sexes. The intakes among non-elderly adults were higher than the elderly adults. The mean intakes of energy decreased with age. The intakes of iron, vitamin A, and riboflavin were less among elderly as compared to non - elderly. Due to low intake of vegetables, food rich in micronutrients and increased susceptibility to infection, anaemia and Vitamin B complex deficiency may be more common in the elderly.

Calcium intake is low across ages in Indian dietaries. Adequate dietary calcium intake from birth to 30 years is critical for the development of peak bone mass which in turn is critical for reduction in age related decline in bone mass and osteoporosis in elderly. With changing lifestyles; outdoor activities and exposure to sun is decreasing. As a result the vitamin D status of all segments of the population is compromised. This renders the elderly more prone to osteoporosis. Osteoporosis occurs more commonly in women than in men as bone loss occurs earlier and more rapidly in women as compared to men. With increasing longevity, it is expected that there will be an increase in the number of persons with osteoporosis. There is currently very little data on the incidence of osteoporosis and osteoporotic fractures. In view of the increasing proportion and number of elderly efforts will have to be made to ensure adequate calcium / vitamin D status in all segments especially among the elderly.

Figure 4: Prevalence (%) of Chronic Energy Deficiency (CED) among Elderly by Age

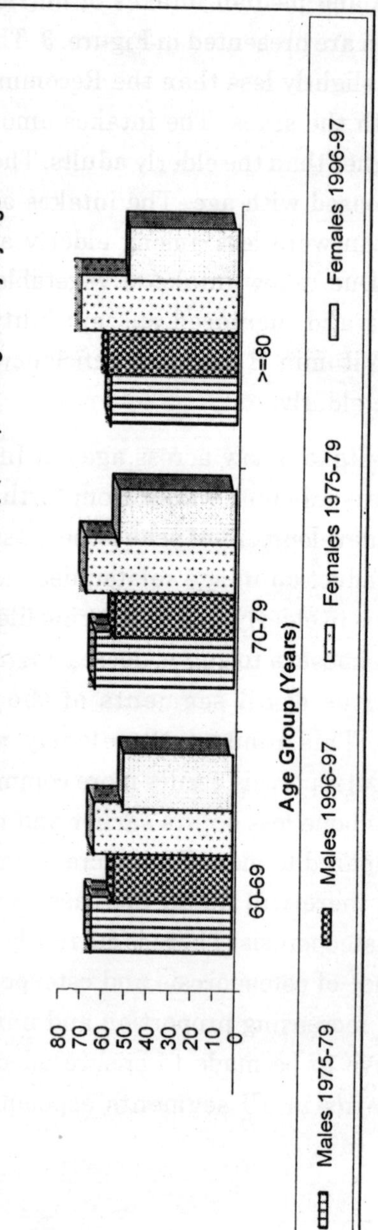

The prevalence of chronic energy deficiency (CED) as assessed by BMI < 18.5 was relatively more among males

Figure 5 Distribution (%) of BMI among elderly and non-elderly - Male

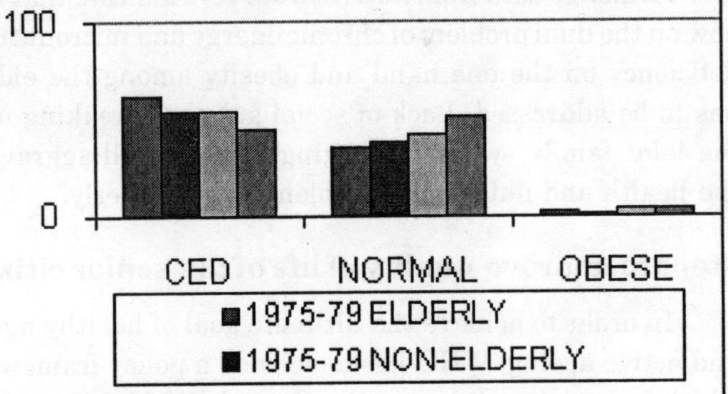

Source: Reference

Figure 6: Distribution (%) of BMI among elderly and non-elderly - Female

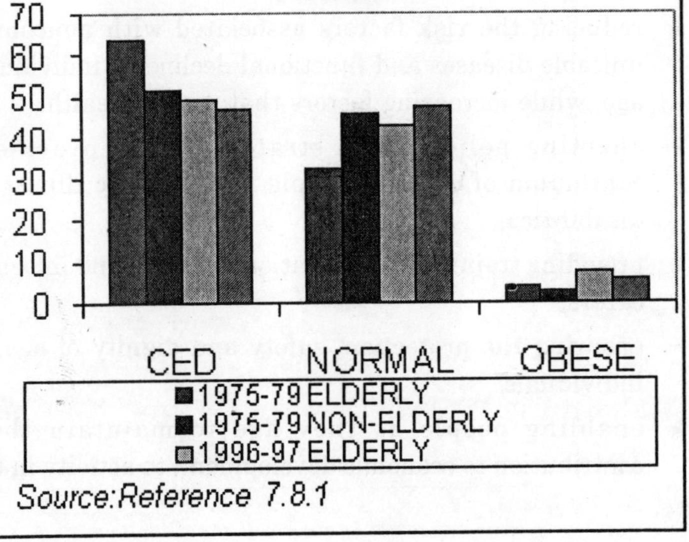

Source: Reference 7.8.1

(53.5%) than in females (49.4%). Over the two decades there is a reduction in the prevalence of CED both in men and women but the reduction is more in women (Figure 4)[2]. The prevalence of overnutrition was higher in elderly men as compared to elderly women (Figures 5 & 6).[2]

Available data from nutrition surveys indicate that from now on the dual problem of chronic energy and micronutrient deficiency on the one hand and obesity among the elderly has to be addressed. Lack of social support, breaking up of the joint family system, changing lifestyles all aggravates the health and nutritional problems of the elderly.

Steps to improve quality of life of the senior citizens

In order to achieve the ultimate goal of healthy ageing and active ageing, WHO has developed a policy framework, which it introduced during the Second World Assembly on Ageing (Madrid, 8-12 April 2002). The framework focuses on such areas as:

- preventing and reducing the burden of disabilities, chronic disease and premature mortality;
- reducing the risk factors associated with noncommunicable diseases and functional decline as individuals age, while increasing factors that protect health;
- enacting policies and strategies that provide a continuum of care for people with chronic illness or disabilities;
- providing training and education to formal and informal carers;
- ensuring the protection, safety and dignity of ageing individuals;
- enabling people as they age to maintain their contribution to economic development, to activity in the

formal and informal sectors, and to their communities and families.

In India, the National Policy on Older Persons announced in January 1999 provides a framework for welfare of the elderly persons including improved financial security and increased access to health and nutrition services. It is envisaged that National Plan of Action for the implementation of the policy will be drawn up. The policy also recommends research to expand the knowledge base on nutritional needs of the elderly.

In many states elderly persons who are without any financial support get old age pension. The amount as well as coverage varies between states but, on the whole, the amount provided is too low to meet the nutritional and health care needs of the elderly persons. Following reports of severe under-nutrition among the elderly and destitute persons in several states, the central and the state governments initiated steps to improve the access of these segments to food-grains.

Innovative efforts to provide societal support, health care and nutrition services to the elderly are currently being taken up by several agencies. Simultaneously, there are efforts to improve family and societal support to elderly within the existing cultural ethos in different regions. Successful models for improving quality of life of elderly will have to be replicated.

Food-based Dietary Guidelines

It is important to obtain essential nutrients through a food-based approach rather than depending on vitamin and mineral supplements. The nutrient-based approach to recommended intakes is limited in that it does not consider the environmental, socio-economic and lifestyle context of eating. Nor does it adequately address the chemical complexity of foods and the interaction and synergies, whether between foods or individual food components. In addition to the recognized essential nutrients, there are many other food components about which little is known; they nevertheless can have important- e.g. anti-inflammatory, anti-microbial, anti-oxidant, anti-mutagenic, antiangiogenic or hormonal-biological effects, capable of lowering the risk of major health problems such as cancer and heart disease.

In 1996 FAO and WHO[3] jointly organized a consultation on the development of food-based dietary guidelines as part of the two organizations continuing efforts to increase the relevance and effectiveness of nutritional recomm endations in everyday life. This method takes into account diet and health relationships in a culturally sensitive manner, thereby providing consumers with easier ways to make healthy food choices. The main recommendations, using the food-based dietary guideline approach, are as follows:

- Emphasize healthy traditional vegetable- and legume-based dishes.
- Eat several (5-6) small non-fatty meals. This pattern appears to be associated with greater food variety and lower body fat and blood glucose and lipid levels, especially if larger meals are eaten early in the day.
- Consume fat from whole foods such as nuts, seeds, beans, olives and fatty fish. Where refined fats are necessary for cooking, select from a variety of liquid oils, including those high in ω-3 and ω-9 fats. Avoid fatty spreads.
- where ever possible select nutrient-dense foods such as fish, lean meat, liver, eggs, soy products (e.g. tofu and tempeh) and low-fat dairy products, yeast-based products (e.g. spreads), fruits and vegetables, herbs and spices, whole-grain cereals, nuts and seeds

- Avoid dehydration by regularly consuming, especially in warm climates, fluids and foods with a high water content
- Limit traditional dishes/foods that are heavily preserved/ pickled in salt and encourage the use of herbs and spices
- Enjoy food and eating in the company of others. Avoid the regular use of celebratory foods (e.g. ice cream, cakes and pastries in western culture confectioneries and candies in Malay culture, and crackling pork in Chinese culture.

India is a vast and varied country with a wide variety of food cultures and cuisines A wide variety of traditional cuisines can promote healthy ageing. Several organizations have come up with recommendation on how to improve dietary intake and nutritional status of the elderly in Indian context. One major fact that has to be kept in mind is that the nutritional needs of the elderly have to be met through dietary intake by appropriate modification from within the family food. Taking vitamin and mineral supple-mentation pills is not the right method to ensure that nutrient requirements are met. There is however one exception to this rule. In India dietary intake of habitual diet in most part of the countries do not contain adequate calcium. With increasingly sedentary indoor life habits, the vitamin D status of the entire population is suboptimal. Poor calcium and vitamin D status renders the elderly more prone to fractures which in turn have sever adverse effect of quality of life. Taking all these into consideration majority of physicians in the country recommend calcium and vitamin D supplementation.

It is equally important to ensure that elderly persons continue to be physically active on a regular basis. This will help in reducing the risk of diabetes and cardiovascular diseases and also ensure muscle and joint health which is critical for preventing deterioration in quality of life.

References

1. Registrar General of India Population projections 2001-2026 New Delhi.
2. NNMB National Nutrition Monitoring Bureau. NNMB special report on elderly: National Institute of Nutrition, Hyderabad.
3. WHO Keep fit for life Meeting the nutritional needs of older persons WHO 2002.

Fig.7 Average (% of RDI) Intake of Foodstuffs (g/CU/day) by Period of Survey

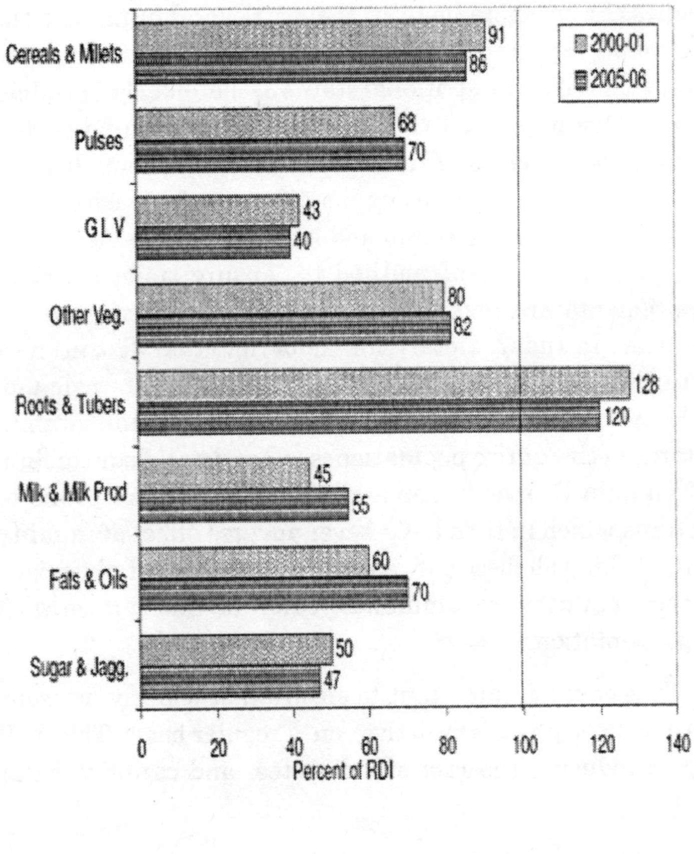

Fig.8 Average (% of RDA) Intake of Nutrients (g/CU/day) by Period of Survey

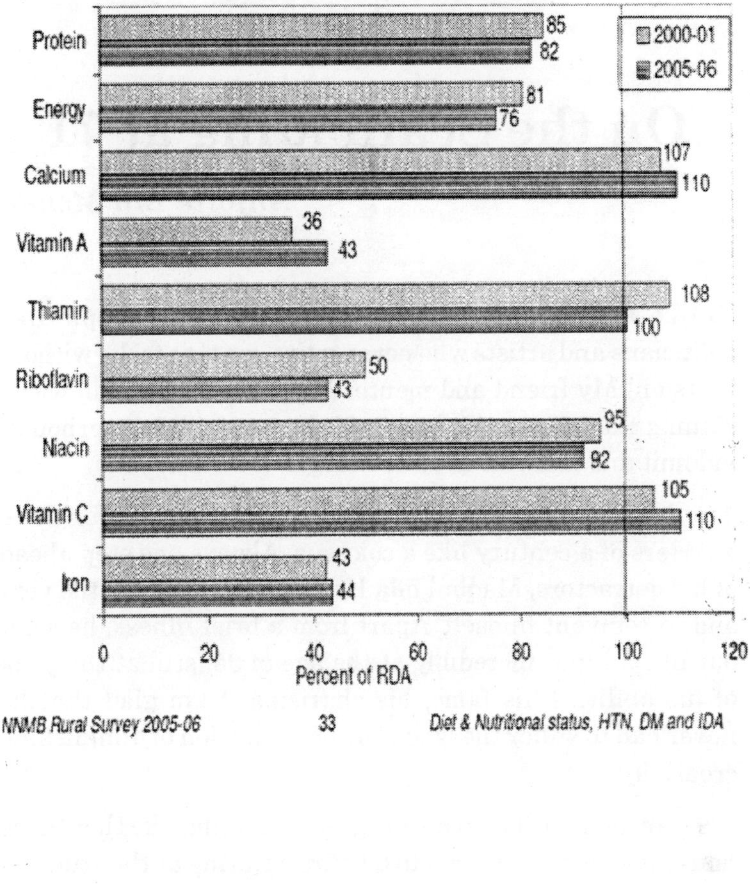

NNMB Rural Survey 2005-06 33 *Diet & Nutritional status, HTN, DM and IDA*

24

On the Scaffolding at 71

Anjolie Ela Menon

Unlike the salaried classes, there are some people like politicians and artists who never retire, we tent to die without boots on! My friend and mentor Maqbul Fida Husain was a shining example to all of us. At 95, he was still a powerhouse, indomitable and full of vital energy.

He strode across the firmament of Indian art for three quarters of a century like a colossus. Always one step ahead of his detractors, Maqbul fida Husain continued till the very end to reinvent himself. Apart from a brief illness, he went out like a light, incredibly at the age of 95, still at the peak of his abilities his fame, his charisma. I am glad that he never had to suffer the ignominy or disillusion of diminishing creativity.

An average day in my life goes something like this. Some household chores, then 5 to 6 hours painting at the studio, a visit to the small NGO for kids which I support in Nizamuddin Basti, meeting and mentoring some young artists and students, time spent with my grandchildren, cooking something for the evening meal, reading or writing after 9.30 pm........ Going to bed a bit guilty for not having exercised today and taking an extra dose of insulin instead!

At 72, I am still happy climbing on a high scaffolding, painting murals. Having worked for 55 years and travelled extensively and changed house (30 times), I am not busy with very large works for public spaces that require a great deal of stamina. I suffer from a number of ailments such as hypertension and diabetes, but I don't let that bother me. As they say if the flesh is weak but the spirit is wiling-one can continue to work, achieve and keep laughing! I dread becoming a complaining hypochondriac....

I am compelled to paint by my inner voice and only pray that the muse will not desert me. The mind is seething with visions and ideas - which only remain to be grasped and made manifest.

Bibliography

1. Davis, T. A. Loyod—Empowering the Elderly.
2. Time: April 25, 2011–Amortality : 'Ageing is the Underdog'.
3. Nature 408: Guarante, Land Keynon, C— Causes of ageing: 'Ageing is the Underdog.'
4. Hagwat Gita: para 3:21—Whatever good people—others also do: 'Ageing Well'.
5. (References relating to the Article: 'Ageism : A Key Factor' by Dr. (Mrs.) Vasantha Parti to be listed at serial nos. 5 {(a) to (m)}. (this issent through a separate file)
6. World Population Ageins : 1995-2050: Dett. of Economic and Social Affairs, Population Division, United Nations, New York—Demographic Profile : 2000-2050 : 'National Policy and Oldest Old in India'.
7. Ashis Bose, 'Our Ageing World : More Ageing than Children' : Power Politics, Vol. III, Issue-12 (January 2011) 'Senior Citizens'.
8. OECD/ World Bank Report : Pensions at a Glance : Asia/Pacific : 'Moving towards Self-Reliance : Pension and Security for the Elderly'.
9. 'Invest India Micro Pension Services' (IIMPS) are promoted (since 2006) by organisations like Sewa Bank, UTI, Dell Foundation – to provide transparently regulated pension products and services to more than 200000 working poor in collaboration with MFIs, cooperatives, worker unions, govt. departments an banks. IIMPS's 'Micro Pension' Model has been has been delivering individual pension and accounts to the poor and motivating them to go in for mass-scale coverage : 'Micro Pension Literacy Programmes and Pension Savings'.
10. World Population Agency : 1950-2050, United Nations — the

Population of those aged 60 and above is expected to increase from 4.6% in 2000 to 9% in 2030. The number of people above the age of 60 will increase from 87.5 million in 2005 to 100.8 million in 2010 and — be over 320 million by 2050. Sanderson & Schebor, Science: 2010 — 'Desability adjusted ageing' : 'Science and Technology for Ageing Population".

11. Phil. Transc. R. Soc, Januar 2011— 'Biological mechanisms underlying pathology'.
12. David Gems : Phil. Trans. R. So : 13, 366, 108-112: 2011— 'Stochastic accumulation of damage to biomolecules-drivers of ageing'.
13. Fontana et al Science 328, 321: 2010: — 'Minimising molecular, cellular and organ damage'.
14. Finch and Taniz: Science 1997, 278, 407-411:— 'Genetic endowment with environmental inflences'.
15. Hjelmberg et all 2006, Hum. Genet. 119, 312-21—'Genetic contribution to human life-span variations'.
16. Bishop, Lu & Yanker : Nature 464, 529, 2010 — 'Dietary restrictions and life-span'.
17. Witte et all PNAS 106, 1255, 2009 — 'Caloric restriction – memory reduction.
18. Fontana et al : Science 328, 321, 2010 — 'Protection against age related pathologies'.
19. Fontana and Klein 2007, Fontana et all 2004 — 'Dietary restriction and obesity'.
20. Levy 2000 — 'Positive attitude towards ageing'.
21. Levy et al 2000— 'Survival advantage and positive self-perception'.
22. Barker DJP : J. Int Med. 216, 412-417, 2007— 'Pathogenesis mechanism and ageing'.
23. Tandon, 2006— 'Technological inputs to maximise function'.
24. References relating to the Article 'Social Protection _ the Informal Economy an Older Women' by Ratna M. Sudarshan to be listed at serial nos. 25 {(a) to (g)}. (to be taken from the bottom portion of the main article and inserted here).
25. The interpretation of substantive equality is based on the Paper: 'The Concept of Substansive Equality and Gender Justice in South Asia' presented by Savitgri Goonesekere at the Sixth South Asia

Regional Ministerial Conference Commemorating Beijing: 17-19 January 2009.

26. Based on data from Annual Reports of Ministry of Defence.
27. The references cited in : National Programme for Health Care of the Elderly : An Initiative towards Active and Healthy Ageing in India are from the documents listed below:
    (a) Census of India (2001).
    (b) Reports of the Registrar General of India.
    (c) National Sample Survey (2004).
    (d) Multi-Centric Study for Health Care Status Needs of the Elderly, GOI-WHO (2007).
    (e) Operational Guidelines on National Programme for Health Care of the Elderly, 2010-11.
    (f) UN Convention on the Rights of Persons with Disabilities (UNCRPD).
    (g) National Policy on Older Persons (NPOP), Government of India, 1999.
    (h) The Maintenance and Welfare of Parents and Senior Citizens Act, 2007 (Section 20) dealing with provisions for medical care of Senior Citizens.

Index

T